EXCELLENCE IN MANAGEMENT

Practical Applications for Success

By
Rick Conlow

Crisp Publications, Inc.
Menlo Park, California

EXCELLENCE IN MANAGEMENT

by Rick Conlow

Credits:
Editor: *Nancy Shotwell*
Typesetting: *ExecuStaff*
Cover design: *Barbara Ravizza*
Artwork: Ralph Mapson

Copyright ©1991 Crisp Publications, Inc.
Printed in the United States of America

Crisp Publications, Inc.
1200 Hamilton Court
Menlo Park, CA 94025

Library of Congress Catalog Card Number 90-85864
Conlow, Rick
Excellence in Management
ISBN 1-56052-103-1

INTRODUCTION

Abigail Adams wrote to Thomas Jefferson in 1790, "These are the hard times in which a genius would wish to live. Great necessities call forth great leaders." These are also hard times in which managers of today face unprecedented challenges such as:

- governmental budget deficits/cutbacks
- world political/economic instability
- energy issues
- environmental problems
- shortages of skilled labor
- higher taxes
- political scandals
- junk bond ripoffs
- culturally diverse work forces
- takeovers
- inflation
- job displacement due to technological advances
- shrinking local markets
- overseas competition
- work ethic concerns

Excellence in Management is in demand today although it is found in short supply. Management gurus abound in giving advice. There are all sorts of theories to pick from. What's a manager to do to be more effective? The bad news is that there isn't any magical formula. The clouds aren't going to part and a heavenly voice won't say, "This is how you do it."

Famed consultant Peter Drucker said, "Don't worry about doing everything right, just do the right things." But, what are the right things? The good news in *Excellence in Management* is that the right things that bring success involve the basics and are learnable.

Excellence in Management is not a theory but an action-oriented book. It includes six key concepts of excellence and 27 proven and practical applications guaranteed to bring you more positive results as a manager. The material evolved from my 15 years of experience in management and sales in the public and private sectors. Over that time I've worked with and trained hundreds of managers. I have implemented what worked and at times what doesn't work. In the last four years, six keys to excellence have emerged that I put into a seminar series called *Excellence in Management*. The chapters of the book parallel the six seminars in the series.

Whether you are a new manager or an experienced one, use *Excellence in Management* as a tool to keep you focused on the skills and techniques of management that make a difference. As you work with the material, you will be required to make a personal commitment to change and grow. Mediocrity is unacceptable in the marketplace today. Even being good isn't good enough anymore. Business is too competitive and the challenges are too great to be content with the status quo. *Excellence in Management* includes the right things to empower you to become one of the "best" in your chosen field.

Rick Conlow
March 1991

*"You'll never be perfect. But aim for perfection
and you'll achieve excellence."*

—Vince Lombardi
Coach, Green Bay Packers (winner of 5 world championships)

CONTENTS _____

Someone once said that when you become a manager you stop doing real work. That's because you no longer make the part, service or repair the part, or sell the part. Instead, you try to get others to assemble the part right, to repair it quickly and properly, and to sell more of it. Management is the process of getting people to do things. It's an influencing and thinking function.

Almost everybody has a story of the worst manager they ever knew. People can also give you an example of the best manager they knew or worked for. Not surprisingly, there are distinct differences. Usually it's easy to spot a poor manager or an excellent one.

In the exercise on the next page, identify the best manager you ever worked for or knew. What did he or she do that made him or her the best? What behaviors or characteristics describe the manager? List the traits on the next page.

Also, think of the worst manager you ever worked for or knew. What did he or she do that made him or her the worst? What behaviors or characteristics describe the manager? List the traits on the next page.

Best Manager Behaviors or Characteristics

1. _____
2. _____
3. _____
4. _____
5. _____
6. _____
7. _____

Worst Manager Behaviors or Characteristics

1. _____
2. _____
3. _____
4. _____
5. _____
6. _____
7. _____

Key Assumptions

1. We know poor or excellent managers when we see one.
2. We know poor or excellent managers by our experiences with one.
3. We know a poor or excellent manager by what they do or don't do.
4. Excellent managers are made, not born.
5. We can learn to do what the best managers do.

Introduction

What do the best managers do?

What do the worst managers do?

Participants at supervisory leadership seminars were asked these questions. The participants were mostly middle managers or people who wanted to be managers. They consistently expressed similar views. The Management Skills Inventory came from their most-often listed behaviors of the best and worst managers.

Rate yourself in these areas on a scale of 1 to 5 (1 = the worst; 5 = the best). In fact, step outside yourself and rate yourself as you think others would rate you. You have nothing to lose, and much to gain by being honest. The rest of the book is dedicated to helping you expand your skills in the best areas.

	The Best	**The Worst**
_____	1. Gives constructive feedback	Gives little or only negative feedback
_____	2. Gives positive strokes	Is critical and abusive
_____	3. Is trustworthy and ethical	Is dishonest
_____	4. Diplomatic	Tactless
_____	5. Supportive	Unavailable
_____	6. Good listener	Poor listener
_____	7. Sensitive	Insensitive
_____	8. Sets clear expectations and goals	Inconsistent about expectations and goals
_____	9. Leads by example	A poor example
_____	10. Follows through	Poor follow-through
_____	11. Good technical ability	Lacks technical ability and won't admit it
_____	12. Strong, but approachable	A dictator

Introduction (continued)

_____ 13. Flexible   Unyielding

_____ 14. Tends to make decisions   Procrastinates often
              and acts

_____ 15. Is a learner   Knows it all

_____ 16. Is a teacher   Can't or won't teach others

_____ 17. Appreciates others   Takes all the credit or
                                                blames others

_____ 18. Is sincere and genuine   Plays politics

_____ 19. Well organized and   Manages by "seat of pants"
              purposeful

_____ 20. Able to delegate   Too controlling

_____ 21. Achieves consistent results   Makes impressive short gains;
                                                fails long term

_____ 22. Confident   Arrogant

_____ 23. Fair   Plays favorites

_____ 24. Positive about company   Negative about company

_____ 25. Expects excellence   Expects perfection or tolerates
                                                mediocrity

_____ 26. Takes reasonable risks   Afraid to take risks

_____ TOTAL

Management Skills Inventory Scale

_130-116_
Your actions make you one of the best. Keep working at it! It's been said the best never rest. Your commitment to excellence makes a difference.

_115-104_
Your impact is good and you're probably achieving fine results. Remember, today good isn't good enough. Use this material for self-improvement.

103 and below
Competition is tough today and challenges are massive. Often the difference between winning and losing is small. This is your opportunity to rise above the crowd and excel. Go for it. There isn't any time to lose.

PART 1

SUCCEEDING AS A LEADER

(How to Supervise in the 1990's)

CASE REVIEW I: The Best or the Worst

Bill was an experienced manager. He had come up through the ranks as a salesperson. He wasn't the top salesperson, but the company always made big profits on his sales. For some reason he always had more than his share of customer complaints, too.

Bill was known as a tough manager. Whenever he took over a department there was a flurry of activity, long hours and results increased. However, sales always tapered off within six months to a year. Bill blamed it on poor people. People in his department called him fair, everyone was subjected to the same verbal abuse. Bill was known for his four letter words. His employees did it "his way or the highway." Turnover was high in his department. Bill's most famous motivational speech was, "Sell 10 units this month or you're fired!"

1. Is Bill one of the best or worst managers? Why?

_____

_____

_____

2. What are three to five character traits you see in Bill?

_____

_____

_____

SET CLEAR GOALS WITH EMPLOYEES

The Philosophy

Goalsetting really works. Few managers do it. If they do, it only involves, "I want you here everyday at work and we'll get along fine!" Showing up for work or being on time is no big deal. If they can't do that, don't hire them, just fire them. Employees need more than that. Employees need goals and a challenge. It helps them perform better. Can you imagine a distance runner running a race not knowing the distance or being timed? Can you imagine playing football without goal lines or keeping track of the score? Ridiculous, you say?

Ask your employees what their goals are. Most won't know or will utter general remarks like:

- to make a living
- to do a good job
- to keep a job
- to make my boss happy
- to survive

If your employees make comments like these, they are not doing their best. It's a manager's responsibility to help employees beyond this barrier to excellence.

The Practice

It's hard work being a manager with employees who lack goals. It's easier being a manager with employees who have goals. Why? Because employees with goals improve their performance. A book entitled *Goalsetting, a Motivational Technique That Works!*, by Locke and Latham, identifies research studies where, in 90% of the cases, goalsetting increased employees' performance. They looked at jobs in typing, keypunch, mass production, and sales. They concluded that goalsetting will, if properly done, motivate employees to increase their efforts. It is the one management technique that works because it establishes expectations and provides a way to give feedback on results. How do you set goals with employees? There are two ways:

- Set the goals for the employee
- Set the goals with the employee

SET CLEAR GOALS (continued)

Either way works, although the second way tends to be more effective. The reason is that the employee is more committed if she has participated in making the goal. She has ownership in the goal and the outcome. When you set goals, set SMART goals. Ken Blanchard and other management consultants recommend this approach.

A SMART goal is defined this way:

> Specific — Is it focused?
>
> Measurable — Can you tell if it is accomplished?
>
> Attainable — Is it a realistic target?
>
> Relevant — Is it a priority?
>
> Trackable — Can the results be compared over time?

Examples:

- Like this: To sell $15,000 in parts the first quarter.
  Not like this: To sell more.

- Like this: To handle all customer complaints within 48 hours.
  Not like this: To satisfy customers.

- Like this: To answer the phone within 3 rings and say: "Good morning, Rosebud Company. This is Mary. How may I help you?"
  Not like this: Do a better job on the phone.

APPLICATION 1

Pick one of your employees and ask her to fill out the goalsetting review sheet. Explain that you will talk to her about it in a couple of days. Then, you fill out the page yourself and when you meet with the employee discuss the information. Over time, talk to an employee about goals on a regular basis. This means monthly, or quarterly at the minimum. Keep in mind, this is not a performance planning and review effort. This is a communication and goalsetting process designed to accomplish these objectives:

1. To create an avenue for the manager and employee to discuss the employee's job duties and performance on a regular basis. And, to do this without the money or salary increases creating unnecessary pressures.
2. To head off problems early, and to give the manager an easy opportunity to give recognition.
3. To focus on goals, not problems, which is a powerful motivating force for both.
4. To give the employee a forum for input into her job, which builds commitment and motivation for a more successful effort.

Note: Throughout *Excellence in Management,* you'll be challenged with "Applications." These are practical and proven management actions that have created positive results for others. Do the applications and you'll initiate a compelling momentum for excellence that will motivate you and others.

Goalsetting Review

Directions: Pick one of your employees that performs well—not the best or the worst. Answer these questions about the employee. Ask the employee to do so on a separate list. Then meet with the employee to discuss both your viewpoints.

1. What are your major job responsibilities/duties?

2. Identify 2 to 3 areas that you perform exceptionally well.

3. Identify 1 to 2 areas that you can do better or improve.

4. What goals (2-5) do you need/want to work towards?

IMPORTANT: Goals are essential to job success. Unfortunately, surveys at leadership seminars find that only 25% to 30% of managers have clearly defined job goals. Your employees need goals and so do you. Fill out a goal-setting review sheet for yourself, too. Later, in the chapter on Achieving Managerial Excellence, Application 27 will give you an opportunity to do this in much greater detail.

Goalsetting Review

1. What are your major job responsibilties/duties?

2. Identify 2 to 3 areas that you perform exceptionally well.

3. Identify 1 to 2 areas that you can do better or improve.

4. What goals (2-5) do you need/want to work towards?

SAMPLE FORM

RECOGNIZE PROGRESS

Motivating people is seldom easy. In fact, many experts say you don't motivate others. You can only create positive conditions so people motivate themselves. Your effort will be more effective though, if you take into account three important conditions. Each condition must be fulfilled—and built upon—before you can move on to the next one.

First, all people want something. They may want more money, a promotion, satisfaction—anything. They must desire it strongly enough to be willing to do something about getting it. As a manager you need to know what it is and turn it into a tangible goal. If people have no goals, no desires, you'll get no motivation from them. Unmotivated employees show little initiative or progress. However, everyone has some motivation. A successful manager will find the "hot button."

Second, they need to know what steps to take to suceed. It does no good to want something when there is no practical, visible way of ever achieving it. When a person has a means or plan for success, they get motivated into action. If they are given the tools and support to succeed, they will. An essential step to motivating anyone is to identify or create the path (bumps and all) that must be traveled. Then a manager needs to help in removing the barriers or smoothing out the bumps.

Third, people must believe that their efforts will be meaningful and rewarded. Many people have goals, know what to do to achieve them, but lack the belief that their efforts will be recognized or have value. This last point makes the goal and effort worthwhile. Recognition is the payoff. Although recognition means different things to different people, it adds fuel to the flame of desire so the motivation continues in spite of the obstacles, which could include the routine of a job.

What Motivates People?

Directions: Rate yourself on what motivates you. Circle the appropriate number. What are the top three motivators for you? Next, can you do this accurately for each employee? If not, find out.

	Very important						Not important
1. Good working conditions	7	6	5	4	3	2	1
2. Awards for being the best	7	6	5	4	3	2	1
3. Money	7	6	5	4	3	2	1
4. Opportunity for growth	7	6	5	4	3	2	1
5. Job security	7	6	5	4	3	2	1
6. Pleasant working conditions	7	6	5	4	3	2	1
7. Interesting work	7	6	5	4	3	2	1
8. Company loyalty	7	6	5	4	3	2	1
9. Feeling involved	7	6	5	4	3	2	1
10. Solving problems	7	6	5	4	3	2	1
11. Self-satisfaction for success	7	6	5	4	3	2	1
12. Goals/achievement	7	6	5	4	3	2	1
13. Contributing to a mission or cause	7	6	5	4	3	2	1
14. Other _____	7	6	5	4	3	2	1

Note: Motivation is individualistic. In order to help motivate someone you have to understand and communicate with that person. Above all, recognize progress, not perfection. Be specific, "Nice job on the report." Just saying "good work," doesn't mean much. Everyone wants some form of recognition. One management survey indicated that 91% of employees wanted recognition. Only 50% felt they got enough. Use positive praise and rewards as the catalyst behind success in your company or department.

APPLICATION 2

Think of your employees or co-workers. See if you can correctly identify what motivates them. Later, talk to your employees about what motivates them. Keep the person's motivations in mind as you communicate with the employee over time. It's the person's "hot button" and is important to remember as you talk about goals and job progress.

How to Recognize Positive Results

Directions: Place a plus (+) sign by all the methods you have used that have worked. Place a check (✔) sign by any method you'll try.

1. Say thank you. _____

2. Take an employee to lunch. _____

3. Compliment publicly. _____

4. Compliment privately. _____

5. Give out trophies for personal best performance. _____

6. Pat an employee on the back. _____

7. Give an employee input into decisions. _____

8. Talk to an employee about his or her family. _____

9. Give a certificate for years of service. _____

10. Share a plaque for sales or service excellence. _____

11. Have an employee of the month. _____

12. Have departments of the month. _____

13. Distribute bonuses for achieving a goal. _____

14. Award an exotic trip for sales or service excellence. _____

15. Put employees' names in newsletters. _____

16. Buy an employee a soda. _____

17. Give dinner certificates for achievement. _____

18. Give an employee a promotion. _____

19. Give an employee a raise. _____

20. Give an employee more responsibility. _____

21. Send the employee to additional seminars or training. _____

22. Hold a recognition dinner or party. _____

23. Put employee pictures on bulletin boards. _____

24. Give out awards for years of service. _____

25. Write the employee a thank you note. _____

26. Other: _____

CONFRONT PROBLEMS

Problems aren't bad. They are inevitable. Without problems you're doomed to fail because you're probably not taking risks as you strive to improve your efforts and results.

Here are five steps to handle common work related problems that arise:

1. Handle it immediately.
2. Be specific about the problem.
3. Explain your feelings about the problem.
4. Outline what you want.
5. Reaffirm the employee.

Handle It Immediately

At this point you're not trying to fire someone. Your goal is to get the employee to stay focused and do the job right. So handle the problem promptly. If your child kept running into the street to play wouldn't you take swift action to stop it? Sure. If an employee has a performance problem, confront it. Why wait? Don't "gunnysack" and save up a month's worth and dump it on the employee. She'll feel threatened and attacked.

Be Specific

Describe the behavior or action that is incorrect. "I saw you punching the button three times instead of two. That's why the part is below tolerance."

Explain Your Feelings

"I'm disappointed that this happened. We've gone over this numerous times." You don't have to scream or use foul language.

Outline What You Want

Then start by asking the employee questions. Is there a system or product problem? Does she need more training? What help is needed? What obstacles are there? Maybe the employee has the idea or information to solve the problem herself. Ask, "How can we avoid this? Where do we go from here?"

By taking this approach, you facilitate the employee solving the problem herself—which she will become more committed to. If the employee doesn't offer much input, explain what you want and expect. Do this in a very nonthreatening manner. Never verbally attack the person. Always follow up and check how your expectations are handled. People will do what you inspect, not just what you expect.

Reaffirm

Tell the employee that you believe in her. Give an example of past success. Do this so the employee focuses on the problem and doesn't feel mistreated.

Note: Only follow these steps with winners. People who know how and can do the job. With trainees or people learning the job, just redirect them. First, point out the error and second, explain and demonstrate what you want. Also, remember to give praise for progress.

APPLICATION 3

Identify an employee who is having performance problems. Write out in advance how you'll confront her. Then do it! Keep in mind, all low performers negatively affect the results of others. It's helpful to do advance planning so the situation is handled properly and the employee is treated with respect.

Common Work-Related Problems

(Check each that you've handled.)

                                                    Yes

 1. Poor performance/productivity   _____
 2. Poor quality work   _____
 3. Abuse of company policy   _____
 4. Theft   _____
 5. Tardiness   _____
 6. Absenteeism   _____
 7. Dishonesty   _____
 8. Customer complaints   _____
 9. Discourtesy   _____
10. Insubordination   _____
11. Critical of other employees   _____
12. Conflict with other employees   _____
13. Poor appearance   _____
14. Lack of follow-through   _____
15. Poor communication with others   _____
16. Sexual/racial harassment   _____
17. Other: _____
18. Other: _____
19. Other: _____

MANAGE WITH FLEXIBILITY

Even though you want to be as fair and consistent as a manager, you can't manage *everyone* the same way. How you manage someone depends on the employee and the situation. Two key questions are:

What is his motivation?
What is his skill?

Your management style shouldn't depend on your personality as much as it depends on the needs of the employee. Ken Blanchard emphasizes the phrase "Different strokes for different folks." Excellent managers realize this.

Management theorists once described management in two camps:

1. Be authoritative, you can't trust employees.
2. Employees are good. Support them.

A manager has to be more well rounded in skill to handle employees in many different scenarios.

For example, if you were a controller, wouldn't you manage an inexperienced accountant differently than a veteran of ten years? Yes! It makes sense, doesn't it?

Notice the chart below. By combining skill and motivation you get four possibilities. (The chart is adapted from Ken Blanchard's and Paul Hershey's *Situational Leadership* and from leadership studies at the University of Ohio.)

Excellence in Management

Flexible Approach to Supervision

The workhorse	The learner
MOTIVATIONAL STYLE	COUNSELOR STYLE
The star	The trainee
RESOURCE STYLE	INSTRUCTOR STYLE

Motivation

Skill

- Motivation—Does the employee want to do the job? Is the employee confident?

- Skill—Can the employee do the job? Is the employee competent?

Style Flexibility Descriptions

1. TRAINEE = INSTRUCTOR STYLE

   Low skill, high motivation (about new job or task)
   - Needs specific training and direction

2. LEARNER = COUNSELOR STYLE

   Some skill, some motivation (declines after initial experience)
   - Needs specific training in some areas; also needs to be motivated to do the job.

3. WORKHORSE = MOTIVATOR STYLE

   High skill, some motivation (most of the time)
   - Needs support and help when not motivated; usually doesn't need specific task help.

4. STAR = RESOURCE STYLE

   High skill, high motivation
   - Needs a resource to kick around ideas, can do the job alone; stay out of his way.

Important:

There is a potential fifth group of employees referred to as deadwood. An employee in this category consistently is a low performer and a problem. What do you do with an employee in this group? *If redirection, coaching and confrontation fails, fire him.*

Often managers are too slow to fire. Remember the mini/max principle. The minimum performance you allow becomes the maximum you can expect. In other words, a low performer negatively affects the performance of others. By following the goalsetting process outlined earlier, you'll be able to detect and deal with low performance more effectively.

Follow your company's policy when you have to fire. Generally most procedures include one or two verbal warnings, and one or two written warnings. Apply the process consistently. Always focus on job performance issues and not generalities like attitude. Document all actions. Firing can be a very delicate area. Do what's right and seek advice from your manager and your company's legal or human resource departments.

Style Flexibility Tips

Motivator Style

- Listen and ask questions
- Give a pat on the back
- Visit one-on-one
- Show concern
- Be readily available
- Review progress periodically
- Discuss progress and goals together
- Handle problems quickly

Counselor Style

- Listen
- Explain
- Demonstrate
- Give helpful suggestions
- Set goals with some involvement
- Answer questions
- Review results/goals
- Give regular positive feedback

Resource Style

- Be available if necessary
- Ask about goals
- Review results
- Give awards
- Challenge the person with new ideas or opportunities
- Ask for opinions and ideas
- Don't get in the way

Instructor Style

- Give specific directions
- Tell how to do it and demonstrate
- Train
- Set goals for the employee
- Supervise closely
- Praise progress
- Redirect on problems

If You Were the Manager... (Answers on page 24)

1. One of your employees feels a little unsure about a job assignment. She is highly skilled and has the talent to do the job very effectively. In the past she has always completed a job well and on time.

   Employee type _____

   Management style _____

   Why?

2. You asked one of your employees to finish compiling the APNONE data file by Friday. The employee usually completes tasks on time with support from you. The file is late.

   Employee type _____

   Management style _____

   Why?

3. One of your employees has seen a dramatic decrease in performance. The employee usually does his job exceptionally well with little help from you. You can't ignore the loss of productivity.

   Employee type _____

   Management style _____

   Why?

4. One of your employees is promoted to manager because of excellent performance. She has little management experience. She's excited about the new opportunity.

   Employee type _____

   Management style _____

   Why?

If You Were the Manager (continued)

5. A new employee is experiencing some difficulty in his job. He performs most of the tasks well but sometimes seems frustrated about various duties and projects.

   Employee type _____

   Management style _____

   Why?

6. You've changed the work schedule of your employee. He is very competent and does his job well with little involvement from you. He was aware of the need for change.

   Employee type _____

   Management style _____

   Why?

7. A new employee seems exceptionally enthusiastic. However, he has a lot to learn. His confidence level is high and is working hard to improve.

   Employee type _____

   Management style _____

   Why?

8. An experienced employee has asked you to meet to discuss a new idea to save expenses. This employee works on his own and usually comes up with positive suggestions that help the whole department.

   Employee type _____

   Management style _____

   Why?

9. You are extremely busy and need help to complete a project. One member of your staff has expertise in the project. She works hard with excellent quality as long as you encourage her.

   Employee type _____

   Management style _____

   Why?

10. An experienced employee with a new job task is running into production problems. He seems irritated at the delays, although he's optimistic about working things out.

    Employee type _____

    Management style _____

    Why?

11. An employee has asked your opinion on a solution to a problem. The employee is highly competent and committed to his job.

    Employee type _____

    Management style _____

    Why?

12. One of your most reliable employees seems quiet lately. The employee usually seems to be willing to talk to you or others. Job results are adequate and consistent.

    Employee type _____

    Management style _____

    Why?

APPLICATION 4

Take time to assess the level of each employee or co-worker you work with. Which type employees are they? How about at different tasks? How should you manage them?

	Overall Level	Management Style
First Person:		
Task A _____	_____	_____
Task B _____	_____	_____
Second Person:		
Task A _____	_____	_____
Task B _____	_____	_____

Diligently practice this management flexibility concept and in time it will become a good habit that you will do unconsciously.

If You Were the Manager... (Answers)

1. **Workhorse • Motivator •** It is a task the employee knows how to do. She needs help with confidence or motivation.

2. **Workhorse • Counselor •** Because she knows how to do it with motivational support from you. Performance is low, step back a style to handle it. Note—when performance dips always step back in your approach.

3. **Star • Motivator •** Because the employee is a top performer with a productivity problem. Step back a style to handle performance problems. Get more involved with the person to find out the problem.

4. **Trainee • Instructor •** Because this is a manager trainee that will need lots of direction/training to succeed.

5. **Learner • Counselor •** Because there is a performance task problem and motivational or emotional issue here. Both areas must be handled.

6. **Star • Resource •** Because the employee can do it and wants to. No real problems. Get out of the way.

7. **Trainee • Instructor •** Because most new employees are highly motivated. However, they need help about job specifics like this one.

8. **Star • Resource •** Because this is a competent and confident employee who wants a listening ear. Do just that.

9. **Workhorse • Motivator •** Because the employee is a reliable employee who needs support to stay effective. Delegate the assignment but be around to assist as needed.

10. **Learner • Counselor •** Because the experienced employee is a learner on a new assignment. Note the mix of attitudes. This employee needs a counselor role.

11. **Star • Resource •** Another star. Listen to his problems, ask questions and give your opinion. Let him decide on a course of action.

12. **Workhorse • Motivator •** Because the employee is dependable and performance seems okay. There is a change in attitude. Be a motivator on this one.

PART 2

COMMUNICATING WITH, PERSUADING, AND INFLUENCING PEOPLE

(How to Create a Positive Impact with Everything You Say and Do)

CASE REVIEW II: The Best or the Worst

Tim owns a major tire manufacturer's franchise. He's worked as a store manager for over ten years at three different locations. Every store he manages turns a profit. He's taken two stores and made losers into winners. Nationally, he always wins performance awards or trips. He is offered promotions, but turns them down because his family is important to him and he doesn't want to relocate.

How does Tim do it? His employees like working for him. He holds regular store meetings for training and motivation. He meets with each employee regularly to talk, set goals and review performance. He buys a birthday cake to celebrate hiring a new employee. When the store reaches major objectives, he'll have a party for employees and spouses to celebrate.

Tim works his employees hard, too. His store is usually open longer than his competitors.

In addition, Tim always has a plan. He's thinking of new incentives for employees or promotions to customers. He does more than the normal corporate line.

When he opened his franchise he asked his employees if they wanted to be professionals and put in the time to make the store work or be hired help and use a time clock. The employees chose to be pros. Soon after, the employees brought spouses and friends to see their new business. Tim's business is taking off and performing better than most new operations.

1. Is Tim one of the best or worst managers? Why?

_____

_____

_____

2. What are five to seven character traits you identified in Tim?

_____

_____

_____

USE THE C.A.R.E. INVENTORY

A major retail company held feedback meetings with its employees to identify problems and solutions. One of the major items on the list was, "We need better communication." The employees defined this to mean:

- let us know about vacation schedules
- teach us more on the products
- talk to us about customer complaints
- have meetings that are constructive
- give us the respect and courtesy that you want us to give to customers

This scenario is not uncommon in businesses or organizations today. One company faced a production quality crisis. Management was having a hard time fixing the problem. A consultant asked if employee input had been used. Management replied, "Why bother?" Another leader of a midwestern company made major changes through a memo. In one instance, a new employee review program was started. No training or meetings were held, only a memo was sent to explain what all supervisors must do. Not surprisingly, a couple of months later only a few employees had been through a performance review.

Communication is a broad term. It can mean many things to many people. Holding a staff meeting once in a while doesn't cut it. All excellent managers communicate, influence and persuade well. Most often it's a priority worked at daily and involves one on one contact with people. It begins by understanding style differences in people's communication patterns.

APPLICATION 5

Complete the inventory on the next page on yourself. Then do it on a person you have trouble communicating with. Are the styles different? What did you learn or relearn? About yourself? The other person?

What I learned or relearned is:

C.A.R.E. Style Inventory

Directions: Work quickly. Select the best description that fits the person listed. Circle the word or phrase that best describes that person in each area.

Name _____

Area			
Interests	status quo	making a good impression	figures/facts	results
Personality	easy going	outgoing	distant	dominating
Eye contact	tentative	warm	glancing	direct
Gestures	reserved	open	closed	impatient
Communication	practical	expressive	controlled	blunt
Voice	unemotional/ low-keyed	emotional/ animated	unemotional/ reserved	emotional/ sharp
Attitude	non-aggressive	trusting	critical	confident
Talking	about current need	about experiences	about details	about results
Listening	willing	drifting	selective	impatient
Responsiveness	controlled	talks freely	unexpressive	short/quick answers
Time orientation	past/present	future	past	present
Concerns	dependability/ cost	color/style	technical/ details	quality/profit
Fears	loss of security	confrontation	criticism	being taken advantage of
Goals	steadiness	good relationships	being right	success
Pace	low energy/ moderate	high energy/ enthusiasm	low energy/ control	high energy/ fast
Decision-making	indecisive	impulsive	methodical	decisive
Dress	traditional	stylish	conservative	formal
Old car style	functional	sporty	appropriate	impressive
Weakness	lack of intensity	organization	people skills	dictatorial
Strength	flexibility	relationships	analysis	gets things done
Totals	_____	_____	_____	_____

C.A.R.E. Style Descriptions

	Conformist	**A**miable	**R**esearcher	**E**xecutive
Strengths	Good listener Draws other out Loyal Patient Team person Supportive	Enthusiastic People oriented Openly expresses feelings Optimistic Confident Promotes ideas	Courteous Sensitive Accurate Concerned about quality Detailed Persistent	Decision-maker Risk takers Prods others to action independent Goal-oriented Change-oriented
Motivators	Appreciation Loyalty Status quo Identification with group Specialization Time limits Security	Recognition People to talk to Freedom from control and details Incentives Helping others Opportunities	No sudden changes Exact job descriptions Reassurance To be part of a group Structure Routine	Achievement Being in control Authority Varied responsibilities Challenges Difficult assignments Prestige
Communication Techniques	Provide a sincere interest in them. Ask questions. Have an exchange of ideas. Have periodic follow-up conversa- tions (this proves your sincerity). Provide reinforcement. Be cooperative. Show patience. Move slowly— check out fears, insecurities. Be patient.	Be stimulating. Present big picture. Use jokes and stories to make a point. Socialize before getting down to the task. Provide professional opinions from people who impress them. Don't dwell on details too long. Asked about their feelings. Get them to outline specifics and time frames. Be friendly.	Be correct. Present facts accurately. Outline the status quo, show the need for a change. Include stats and percentages. Keep your word. Take one step at a time, don't push. Prepare written comparisons. Provide many ex- planations and give them reassurance. Be somewhat formal.	Provide direct answers. Be brief and to the point. Stick to business. Ask questions regarding specifics. Deal with actions and results. Stick with WHAT questions. Don't get bogged down in detail. Be part of the solution, not part of the problem. Provide options and possibilities. Let them choose. Confront them. Don't back down.

Nine Dots Exercise

Introduction: Read the directions and do the exercise below. Try it a number of times. Expand or change your thinking to identify a possible solution that isn't readily apparent.

Directions:

1. Connect all the dots using only four straight lines.
2. No line may pass through the same dot more than once.
3. Don't lift your pencil from the paper.

To succeed as a manager, don't do what all other managers do. Get outside the dots; don't stay within the mold.

One manager of a large electrical company made this comment after a Leadership Seminar. "I asked the other managers at our company about the concepts we learned and produced in class. I asked if they knew how to set goals, problem-solve with people, lead others through style flexibility, etc. The other managers said they knew some of it. But, you know what? They don't use it."

Knowledge is not power. Applied knowledge is power.

To become an excellent manager you have to be willing to do what others never do or only do some of the time. Remember these words of motivator Zig Ziglar, "The greatest enemy of excellence is good."

COMMUNICATION CLIMATE

Whenever two people meet there is a communication climate that exists between them. Sometimes it's positive and other times negative.

The climate can be like the weather. There are distinct signs that give you clues to what's happening. For example, if it's a cloudless day, about 80 degrees, with a 5 to 10 mph breeze, do you get a picture of what kind of day it is? On the other hand, if the day has high humidity, with the temperature falling rapidly from the high 90's to the low 80's, it's dark, and there are fast spinning clouds filling the sky, do you know what is happening?

Communication climate does exist, and it affects how people communicate. It's more behavioral oriented than attitudinal because it is caused by what people do. Again, it can turn out to be positive or negative. The good news is, since it is caused by what people do, it can be managed.

For example, let's say you're talking to a subordinate about a personal problem. You never make eye contact and you talk to her while reading a report. What do you think the employee will feel?

Or let's say you're talking to a customer. You welcome him cordially, offer him a cup of coffee, sit at a round table, make appropriate eye contact and discuss his needs. Do you think the results have a chance to be more favorable than in the earlier example?

Nine Dots Review: Answer

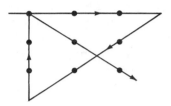

Your Communication Climate

Consciously or subconsciously you do things that contribute to the communication climate you create with any individual.

Here are 5 keys:

1. What you do is of utmost importance. You can't control what the other person does. You can control what you do.
2. Some of your behaviors are positive.
3. Some of your behaviors are negative.
4. In each case, you don't always know what you do that makes a difference.
5. By becoming more aware of what contributes to a positive or a negative climate, you can make changes to be more effective.

APPLICATION 6

In the exercise on the next page, read and visualize how each action can affect communication. In the blank spaces, add other items from your experiences. Then circle five items in the positive column you must always do. Circle three items in the negative column you must stop doing. How can you eliminate these negatives today? How can you use your strengths more effectively? Write your responses below.

Communication Climate Checklist

Positive	Negative
1. Listened (restated problem)	1. Lacked eye contact
2. Good eye contact	2. Acted hostile
3. Talking on the same level—as an equal	3. Allowed interruptions
4. Allowed no interruptions	4. Had physical barriers, such as a desk
5. Gave full and prompt attention	5. Answered questions with a question
6. Asked questions	6. Looked at watch
7. Smiled	7. Acted defensive
8. Used firm handshake	8. Didn't smile
9. Gave compliments	9. Slouched body
10. Was courteous	10. Used monotone voice
11. Stood and sat straight	11. Showed no sincerity
12. Was enthusiastic	12. Didn't follow through
13. Made a decision	13. Used bad language
14. Stayed on subject	14. Was sarcastic
15. Used positive verbal cues	15. Had poor appearance
16. Eliminated barriers	16. Rushed the problem/person
17. Did something extra	17. Told personal problems
18. Stayed positive	18. Criticized others
19. Other _____	19. Other _____
20. Other _____	20. Other _____

LISTEN EFFECTIVELY

Successful salesman, businessman and motivator Bob Conklin says, "To listen you must want to listen." That's the first ingredient. Do you care enough to pay attention?

All excellent managers are good listeners. They take time to hear the problems of subordinates, co-workers, or customers.

There are many barriers to effective listening. Here are a few of them (put a ✓ by those that affect you in your attempts to listen effectively):

- noise distractions
- interruptions
- differences of opinion
- prejudices, biases
- different priorities
- busyness
- no interest
- limited time
- thinking of other things
- thinking someone is wrong
- tiredness
- perception differences

Listening can be tough work. Unfortunately, few managers or people in general know how to listen effectively. Often the only reason employees say they don't feel appreciated is because no one listens properly. The lack of listening and poor communication skills cost businesses millions of dollars a year in performance and morale problems.

How to Listen

As stated earlier, first you have to want to listen. However, there are other techniques that help. Each are described below:

- Make eye contact.
- Use positive body language.
- Use the person's name.
- Paraphrase what's said.

Eye Contact

In our society we don't lock eyeballs; that's intimidating. We use the glance-away method instead. Look at your partner for 3 to 4 seconds, then quickly look down or to the side. Then make eye contact again. Proper eye contact expresses interest and empathy. One consultant is so adroit at this that her co-workers and customers call it uncanny. Anyone who talks to her feels special and that they really matter.

Body Language

Lean forward and in towards the employee. Face the person directly. Don't fold your arms. Keep them on your lap or desk. Take notes if appropriate. (Tell the employee before you do). Put your feel flat on the floor. Use this approach in the beginning to express your concern and willingness to be involved.

Person's Name

Use it. The sweetest sound to anyone is their name. By using their name you demonstrate a positive relationship and interest. You'll also get the person's attention.

Paraphrase

At an appropriate time (whenever you feel you're receiving too much information to remember or understand) in the conversation, repeat to the person what she told you. Use your own words, of course. Start a paraphrase like this:

"If I understand you correctly . . . "
"What I hear you saying is . . . "

Don't say bland phrases like, "I understand." This isn't a paraphrase. Also, avoid saying, "What you really mean is _____ ." This is nothing more than an attempt to put words into someone's mouth or interpret someone's statement.

The Goal of Listening

By listening to someone you are not necessarily agreeing with them. The major goal of the listening technique is to better *understand* the employee. And, during that process, to express interest and concern in the employee's problem or idea.

APPLICATION 7

How do you rate on the Listening Quiz? Be honest and go to work on improving your listening skills. You'll become a better manager, parent, friend, and spouse, too. Fill out the listening quiz. Then have an employee, co-worker, and perhaps a spouse fill it out on you. What did you learn or relearn?

Listening Checklist

Directions: Rate yourself on a scale of 1-5 for each item. 1 = poor;
5 = excellent.

_____   1. Do you want to listen?

_____   2. Do you put what you are doing out of sight and out of mind?

_____   3. Do you make eye contact?

_____   4. Do you ignore or eliminate distractions?

_____   5. Do you smile, nod your head, and otherwise encourage the other person to talk?

_____   6. Do you think about what you will say?

_____   7. Do you try to figure out what the other person means through clarification?

_____   8. Do you try to figure out why the person is saying it?

_____   9. Do you let the other person finish what he or she is trying to say?

_____ 10. If the person hesitates, do you encourage him or her to go on?

_____ 11. Do you restate or paraphrase what the person says and ask if you got it right?

_____ 12. Do you withhold judgment about the idea or problem until the person is finished?

_____ 13. Do you listen regardless of the person's manner of speaking and choice of words?

_____ 14. Do you listen even though you anticipate what the person is going to say?

_____ 15. Do you question the person in order to get him or her to explain the idea more fully?

_____ 16. Do you ask what is meant by some words to eliminate misunderstanding later?

How Well Do You Listen?

80-70   Excellent! . . . You do a fine job of listening!

69-59   Your efforts are positive and done well.

58-48   Some areas are fine and above average. Pick a few to work on.

47 or less Listening is a skill that can be learned. Practice to improve. It will make a difference in your communication with others.

BUILD TRUST AND RAPPORT

Building trust and rapport is about getting along with other people. It's not something that people seem to work at, yet most people feel they are good at it.

A speaker at a convention asked his audience members to stand if they couldn't get along with other people. No one stood up. Finally, after some silence a young man stood up in the back of the room. The speaker asked, "Young man, you mean to tell me that you can't get along with other people?" The man replied, "Oh, sure I can. But I felt sorry for you standing up there all by yourself."

People don't get along because they don't work at it or don't know how. They are also selfish, looking out for number one. Remember the bumper sticker, "He who dies with the most toys wins." So what's the answer for a manager who desires to motivate or influence others?

Excellence in Communicating

Successful communication starts with an attitude. Then there are four key skills that help.

Author and motivator Zig Ziglar declares, "Give other people what they want and you'll get what you want." Notice how he said this. First, you give, then you get. It isn't the other way around. This attitude is based on the Golden Rule. And yes, it is a concept that applies in any organization. Tom Peters, who co-wrote the book, *In Search of Excellence,* declares that they tried to identify policies, structures, and procedures that made a company great. Instead, they found intangibles—enthusiasm, pride, respect, caring, fun, and love. If you want to communicate effectively with people you have to change your approach by giving more. However, there are specific skills you can learn to get along better or to motivate more.

Before those skills are reviewed, do the exercise on the next page.

The Difficult and Different Person Exercise

Directions: Think of a person you have a hard time communicating with. This could be someone with different values or ethnic background. Or, it could be someone with whom you've had strong differences in the past. In the outline below, describe that person with as much detail as you can.

1. Interests/hobbies:

2. Career/job:

3. Strengths:

4. Weaknesses:

5. Physical description:

6. Likes/dislikes:

7. Voice:

8. Mannerisms:

9. Background/education:

10. Family:

Three Rules for Rapport

1. People who are like each other tend to like each other and tend to work well together.
2. People who are unlike each other tend not to like each other and tend not to work well together.
3. Be genuine.

The Difficult or Different Person

Whenever two people communicate, who is responsible to create positive communication? Both people? That's the textbook definition. In reality you are 100% responsible. You can't control what others do, but you can control what you do. Your actions will greatly influence the other person.

For example, with this difficult/different person, do you catch yourself in these scenarios:

- avoiding the person
- criticizing the person openly
- criticizing the person to yourself
- being defensive right from the start
- dreading the next encounter
- replaying in your mind past negative communication
- preplaying in your mind a negative end result the next time you meet
- Judging whether or not his/her lifestyle is right

Were you able to accurately describe the other person? Most people can't. Perhaps by changing your preparation, you can communicate more effectively. In the work force, there are increasing levels of cultural diversity. To work effectively with these differences you'll need to adapt. Excellent managers take the initiative to change their approach to better understand others. Besides listening, use of the skills of trust and rapport will help you.

In addition, excellent managers master the following skills of matching or mirroring. Matching or mirroring is the process of becoming like the person you are talking to.

Skills of Trust and Rapport

1. Common ground
2. Body language
3. Voice tone
4. Mood
5. Concerns/problems

Common Ground

A very successful salesperson once explained his success this way: "I find common ground or interest with everyone. If people like fishing, we talk about it. If they are into sports, so am I. If they are older, I become the long lost son. I'm like a chameleon."

A key to influencing others is establishing connections through common ground or interest. Do you know the things that interest your employees? How about that difficult/different person? We've already seen with the CARE inventory how important this is.

Body Language

A study indicated the three items that affect the result of communication the most.

- words
- voice tone
- body language

What percentage falls in each area? Words account for 7% of your communication impact. Voice tone equals 38%. Body language influences the outcome 55%. Isn't that amazing?

What you say is one thing. How you say it is more significant. What you do about what you say is most powerful.

To match someone's body language, sit as she sits. Cross your arms if he does. Mirror the gestures and shifts in position. *Never mimic, do everything subtly!* It'll make an impact that says, "You can trust me, I'm like you!"

Voice Tone

This skill is helpful, too. Observe and listen to the person you talk to. Does she speak fast or slow? Does she speak in short sentences or long ones? Does she have a low voice or a high one? Adjust your voice tone to be similar.

Skills of Trust and Rapport *(continued)*

Mood

This is especially critical with an angry person. Become angry yourself. Don't be angry at the person. Match the intensity of the mood. Show immediate concern and a desire to take action. Acknowledge that the person has a right to be upset and that you'll get on it. There is a proverb that says, "He who is cheerful in the morning is counted as a curse." In other words, if two people's moods don't match, chances are they won't communicate well.

Concerns/Problems

When a person has a problem, agree with it, at least initially. Don't argue. Try to understand the person's point of view. Say something like this: "I agree that in some situations that makes sense. At other times another approach may get more favorable results. For example . . ."

You actually partially agree or agree on minor points. This builds rapport and creates a desire in the other person to hear your point of view or information because you acknowledged hers.

APPLICATION 8

How does this relate to management?

These five skills are ways to build individual credibility, establish teamwork and win over difficult or different people. Each has to be applied in daily situations to be effective. However, each skill can *rapidly* improve results and relationships. Do the exercise below.

In the next week, practice and practice these skills. Note your observations and results. If at first it seems nothing happens, do the exercise below again.

Change Exercise

Step 1.   Clasp your hands together.
Step 2.   Note which thumb is on top.
Step 3.   Clasp your hands together again with the other thumb on top.
Step 4.   How does it feel? Awkward? Uncomfortable?
Step 5.   Whenever you try something new or different the first few times, that's the result you get. If you're really motivated to change and improve, with patience and practice, you'll learn to do a skill automatically and with confidence.

MAKE MEMORABLE PRESENTATIONS

A study asked Americans what they feared most. Number one on the list was speaking in front of a group. Number seven on the list of ten was death. People would rather die than get up in front of a group of people and talk.

All managers at one time or another either lead a meeting or give a speech. How it is done affects the overall impact of their communication with employees. There are two keys to making memorable presentations—preparation and practice.

Preparation

Lack of experience and skill can be overcome with preparation. Run effective meetings by:

1. Communicating ahead of time.
2. Having an agenda.
3. Starting on time, ending on time.
4. Studying the materials.
5. Sticking to the agenda/task.
6. Getting others involved through task reports, assignments on agenda items or questions/answers.

Brian Tracy, sales consultant and author, suggests, "Winning isn't everything, the will to prepare to win is everything."

How to Prepare a Presentation

Here are three basic methods to follow when preparing the presentation and then giving it.

The Outline Method

For example:

Budget expenses:
A. Administrative
    1. paperwork
    2. supplies
    3. temporary help

How to Prepare a Presentation (continued)

B. Sales
   1. entertainment
   2. sales aides
   3. bonuses
C. Customer Service
   1. policy adjustment
   2. training

The Point Method

For example:

Keys to success
- teamwork
- positive attitude
- goals
- discipline

Question Method

For example:

Computer Technology
- How is it affecting our business today?
- How will it affect us tomorrow?
- What action should we take?

Summary

Each of these methods represents a way of presenting information. Each can be effective. Use them by first writing out what you have to say. Then practice. See the exercise on the next two pages.

In each, remember to use these three powerful steps.

Introduction
1. Tell the audience what you'll tell them.
2. Key ideas—Tell them.
3. Summarize—Tell them what you told them.

Finally, support your presentations with facts, figures, stories, humor, analogies, and visuals. As you do, you'll increase the interest in others of what you have to say.

APPLICATION 9

Here is a list of ways to improve your presentations.

Put a + sign by any item you've already used. Circle the items you'll use to develop your skills in presenting.

_____ 1. Talk into a dictaphone or tape recorder.

_____ 2. Join Toastmasters.

_____ 3. Present your talk in front of a mirror.

_____ 4. Rehearse while driving home.

_____ 5. Read aloud to your children.

_____ 6. Volunteer to talk to community groups.

_____ 7. Attend a seminar or class.

_____ 8. Listen to a cassette tape series on speaking.

_____ 9. Read a book on speaking.

_____ 10. Give a presentation to your family or friends.

_____ 11. Write the presentation word for word and read and reread it.

_____ 12. Join an acting group.

_____ 13. Other idea: _____

_____ 14. Other idea: _____

APPLICATION 10

Prepare a memorable presentation. In the space below, prepare your next presentation or talk. Use one of the methods discussed earlier.

PART 3

CREATING SUPERIOR SERVICE

(How to Gain the Key Competitive Edge)

CASE REVIEW III: The Best or the Worst

The president of a company in a major metro market that owns car dealerships decided to improve customer service at his stores. He noticed the industry's need to change its image. He also felt the increased demands of the customer and the competition. His dealerships were below average to average in taking care of the customer. Over a four-year period, the company gained national recognition and market leadership in customer satisfaction in every product line sold.

Excellent results were achieved by following *seven* basic steps:

1. Establishing commitment from management. This took many meetings and training sessions.
2. Gaining employee involvement and feedback through surveys, training and employee councils.
3. Surveying customers regularly to identify needs and concerns.
4. Educating employees about the importance of quality and training them on needed customer contact skills.
5. Recognizing and rewarding positive results.
6. Problem-solving specific and recurring problems through joint management/employee involvement.
7. Starting over to stay focused, enthusiastic and a step ahead of the competition.

The president of the company invested money and effort to achieve the goal of being the best through continuous improvement. More importantly, he was absolutely committed to increasing customer satisfaction.

During an economic slowdown, this company continued to be profitable while competitors started losing money and, in some cases, went out of business. One store achieved these results in a year: Sales rose 9% in a market that was down 10%. Advertising costs were down 30% too. However, customer satisfaction and repeat/referral results were at all-time highs.

1. Is this company president one of the best or worst managers? Why?

_____

2. What can you learn/relearn from the case study that applies to the service your department or company gives?

_____

UNDERSTAND THE VALUE OF QUALITY

A manager's success depends on results. Customer satisfaction is a quantifiable result, just like sales or profit. Why provide excellent service or quality? Quite simply, the success or failure of your business will be determined by your success in satisfying customer needs. A major fatal error managers make today is not understanding the value of customer satisfaction and how it relates to their departments. Everyone in a company is responsible for superior service and quality.

Key Facts

- A satisfied customer will tell four to five other people.
- A dissatisfied customer will tell eight to ten other people. Many tell twenty or more.
- Approximately one in four of a business' customers has complaints. An average business never hears from 96% of these customers.
- Over 95% of these complaints can be handled satisfactorily. These customers tell an average of five other people.
- It costs five times as much to get a new customer as it does to keep an old customer.

Today's Challenge

Many businesses prosper or fail based on word of mouth alone. The word travels fast if you are the best at meeting customer needs and it travels even faster if your service is bad.

IBM has been the leader in the business machines industry not because it builds the best computers or copiers, but because it provides the best service when one of its machines breaks down.

Joe Girard, world famous car salesman, says, "Let me sell you a lemon so I can show you how good my service department is."

There is no faster way to develop loyal long-term customers than to be there when a problem develops to see that it is solved to the customer's satisfaction. Likewise, there is no quicker way to drive customers away than to put them off or try to blame the problem on them. Customer service can cost you in the short term but will pay you tremendous dividends in the long term.

Today's Challenge (continued)

You need to devote yourself, not only to record-breaking effectiveness, but also to excellence in customer service.

The challenge will increase in the 1990's for these reasons:

Service focus
Although the U.S. is still an industrial giant, 66% of all jobs and businesses relate to services. Today the U.S. has a service economy. What are your strengths/weaknesses in service?

Education
Customers are more sophisticated today through increases in education. Customers also expect better treatment and quality as a result of consumer advocate groups. How can you better educate customers? employees?

Competition
If you haven't noticed, competition is increasing at home and abroad. Customers can go anywhere to buy clothes, shoes, cars, food, jewelry, homes, and appliances. Have you seen any businesses fail recently? What makes you better, faster, or different than your competition? In the 1960's, 20% of American products had foreign competition; in the 1990's, nearly 70% did and internal competition is a way of life today.

Economic Sense
Customer satisfaction positively affects profits. The Strategic Planning Institute found that companies with the best customer satisfaction had an average ROI of 30% to 35%; the poor service providers' average was 10% to 12%. Ford Motor Company found that its best service dealers significantly out-performed the poor service dealers in market share and repeat/referral business. Whether you serve the consumer or a co-worker, how can you improve to help your company become more profitable?

Strive for Excellence

There are three basic levels of customer satisfaction in the marketplace today.

1. Expedient
2. Adequate
3. Excellent

Where is your company? Your department? Where do you want to be as a manager? And, what is excellence, anyway?

Expedient

Companies in this category care only about the money. They aren't interested in you, the customer. The products are poor quality and service is bad. The movie, "Tin Man," displayed the behavior of expedient salespeople. Recently, stock brokers have gone to jail for ripping off the public with junk bonds. Have you spent money with an expedient company lately? Do you want to go back? About 10% of businesses fall into this category.

Adequate

Businesses at this level believe in customer service. They have departments to handle complaints. Meetings are held occasionally; buttons are handed out, and posters displayed. Go to Anymall, USA and you'll receive adequate service in the different stores. Their goal is to sell something and to satisfy you. They are fairly good at it. About 80% of American businesses fall into this category. This is average and it isn't enough to ensure success.

Excellent

Adequate isn't good enough. The competition is too tough; the economy too unpredictable to be like everyone else. The customer is king today! The excellent companies and managers know this. What do they do? They intensively follow the seven steps in Case III. Only 10% of companies make the commitment to be excellent. Although there isn't any magic to their efforts, it does require a passionate, sometimes zealot-like commitment to be the best. The goal of excellent companies is to more than satisfy the customer.

SURVEY CUSTOMER NEEDS

APPLICATION 11

Analyze your department or company as follows:

Customer Satisfaction Analysis

1. *Service Focus*

Strengths	Weaknesses

2. *Education*

Customers—

Employees—

3. *Competition*

Better—

Faster—

Different—

4. *Economic Sense*

Ideas for Improvement

a.

b.

c.

APPLICATION 12

Part I   Service Excellence Checklist

Do the checklist below. What level are you? Be prepared to use this information in an action plan later in this chapter.

Service Excellence Checklist

	Yes	No
1. Are you 100% committed to Customer Satisfaction Excellence?	___	___
2. Do all your employees understand the importance of Customer Satisfaction?	___	___
3. Do you regularly (at least monthly) survey customer needs?	___	___
4. Is Customer Survey data reviewed with all employees?	___	___
5. Do you have a written Customer Satisfaction plan that is updated quarterly?	___	___
6. Do all employees receive Customer Satisfaction skill training?	___	___
7. Are all employees recognized and rewarded for superior service?	___	___
8. Are all employees involved in identifying and solving problems to help improve service?	___	___
9. Do all employees know and understand your strategy/plan for service?	___	___
10. Is Customer Satisfaction reviewed/discussed at department meetings just like sales or profit or some other departmental priorities?	___	___
11. Do all employees have PRIDE in their service results?	___	___

APPLICATION 12 (continued)

Evaluation

10-11   Excellent! You're on the right track. You're probably doing many other things exceptionally well. Keep at it diligently!

7-9   Adequate. Most companies do as well. Just as 1/10th of a second can lose a race for a sprinter, little things mean a lot in service. The difference between winning and losing is slight. No detail is too small to overlook.

below 7   Expedient. You've got to do more to survive today.

Part II   What is Excellence?

Imagine that when you go to work tomorrow you are the customer, not the employee. The reason you're going to your business is because it provides excellent service. What would your company have to do for you as a customer to bring you back? Think of what it would take. List seven to ten characteristics of the business and the behaviors of the employees that would demonstrate excellence. Include how the place looks, how you would be treated, how people work together, employee attitudes, etc. You'll notice that you understand excellence from your experiences and memories. This happens to your customers, too.

What Is Excellence?

Characteristics/behaviors of excellence

1.

2.

3.

4.

5.

6.

7.

8.

9.

10.

MANAGE THE "MOMENTS OF TRUTH"

Jan Carlson, CEO of Scandinavia Airlines, coined this term. He took charge in 1981 when SAS was losing $20 million that year. One year later, SAS earned $54 million. How did he do it? He took a customer-focused approach to better manage, as he says, "50,000 daily 'Moments of Truth'" with the customer.

Every business or department has thousands of "Moments of Truth." A "Moment of Truth" is defined as any direct or indirect customer contact. Here are some examples:

- how a phone is answered
- how fast a phone is answered
- cleanliness of the restroom
- date on the magazines in a customer lounge
- appearance of the employees
- appearance/cleanliness of the business
- use of signs
- company stationery
- how a complaint is handled
- how quickly a complaint is handled
- how routine customer questions are handled
- what employees say to one another
- if employees are pleasant and if they smile
- how employees work together
- how promptly customers are helped or served
- how a promise is handled
- how a product defect is handled
- what happens after the sale

Moments of Magic or Misery

Phil Wexler, consultant and salesperson, told Ford Motor Company that a moment of truth "can be identified as magic or misery." A "moment of magic," for example, means that the employee performed a "moment of truth" with that extra touch. The customer feels she received more than expected. A "moment of misery" begins when a customer's expectations aren't met. She feels let down or mistreated. Customer satisfaction occurs when the "moments of magic" far exceed the "moments of misery." Excellence occurs when the "moments of magic" become a way of life for the department or company.

Moments of Truth Exercise

Directions: Brainstorm 15 to 20 of the moments of truth in your department or business. Write them by the dashes in the circle. Then, identify 3 to 5 that are usually moments of magic and moments of misery. Write them in the space below.

Moments of Truth

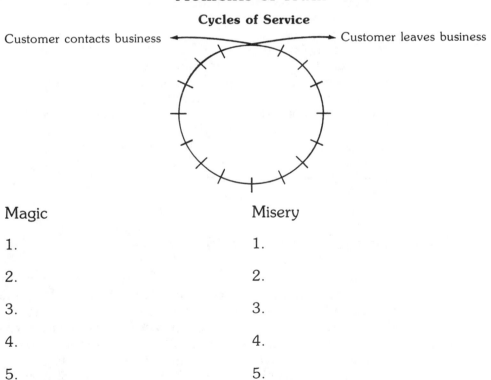

Cycles of Service

Customer contacts business ← → Customer leaves business

Magic	Misery
1.	1.
2.	2.
3.	3.
4.	4.
5.	5.

FOLLOW THE SERVICE MODEL

All employees of a company need intensive customer service training for three major reasons:

1. To understand company commitment and philosophy to service excellence.
2. To learn or relearn skills or procedures to be effective.
3. To refocus their attitudes and commitment to service.

There are three key areas of "moments of truth" that significantly affect the satisfaction level of the customer. These broad areas are:

- Greeting
- Meeting the need
- Following up

Usually, service personnel are good at meeting the need. They know the policy or procedure and follow it. Or, they understand the technical aspect of the product and can explain it. Service personnel often fail at the greeting and following up areas because these areas involve more time and attention. That's where a department or a company can distinguish itself.

APPLICATION 14

Hold a meeting with your employees. Review the "moments of truth" concept. Distribute a copy of the Customer Service Model. Ask the employees to write on the service model sheets and identify the key moments of truth for their jobs. Discuss the results for a couple of positions. Distribute and review the Customer Service Model sample. Tell the employees that you will meet with each of them soon to review the Customer Service Model. At the end of the meeting, review the negatives and positives of any customer surveys or feedback you've received.

Customer Service Model

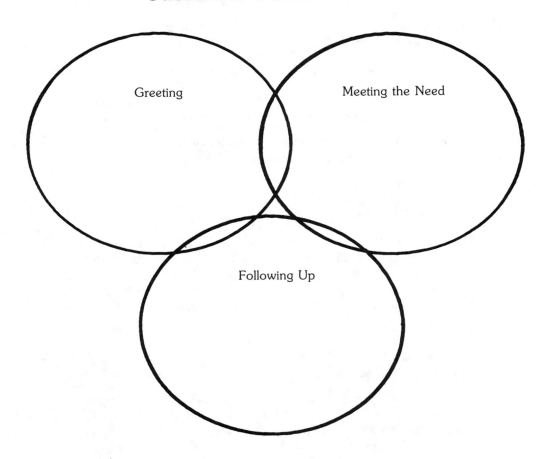

Customer Service Model:

Greeting the Customer

1. Smile
2. Say, "Welcome to _____"
3. Be friendly (if appropriate, talk non-business)
4. Ask, "How may I help you?"
5. Be courteous (use their name, give your name, say, "Please," "Thank you)"

Meeting the Need

1. Listen
2. Restate need
3. Ask questions to clarify
4. Offer options/alternatives
5. Apologize, if appropriate
6. Get agreement and act
7. Summarize

Following Up or Following Through

1. Say, "Thank You!"
2. Send follow-up note
3. Make follow-up call
4. Double check order
5. Ask for additional business
6. Do something extra
7. Survey the customer

Create Added Value for Your Customers

"Before you test yourself against the competition, strategy takes shape in the determination to create value for customers."
—Kenichi Chimae (head of McKinsey's office in Tokyo)

To create value for customers you need to ask, "What makes me and my company so special? Why would our customers want to keep doing business with us or feel good about us?"

Leonard C. Berry of Texas A & M University identified five key dimensions of service quality:

Reliability—Ability to perform promised service accurately and dependably.
Assurance—Courteous and knowledgeable employees who project trust/rapport to customers.
Empathy—Overall caring attitude and individual attention to customers.
Tangibles—Appearance of employees and the company.
Responsiveness—Ability to provide prompt service and willingness to help customers solve problems.

Research by the Forum Corporation suggests customers rank the importance of these items as below.

1. Reliability
2. Responsiveness
3. Assurance
4. Empathy
5. Tangibles

Forum Corporation also asked customers how companies perform in these areas. Here are the results:

1. Tangibles
2. Assurance
3. Responsiveness
4. Empathy
5. Reliability

Isn't it interesting that companies aren't performing well in the areas that customers want service, especially in responsiveness and reliability? You can take advantage of this and make service your competitive advantage.

Value Plus Customer Service

Directions: Put a + by each behavior your company or department does well. Put a − by each behavior you do poorly. Use this information to improve your service.

1. Pays compliments to customers. _____
2. Has a preferred customer program. _____
3. Sends thank-you letters to customers. _____
4. Documents complaints and follows all problems to completion. _____
5. Offers customers options for service. _____
6. Has fun with regular customer (no cost) promotions. _____
7. Recognizes customers we've served before. _____
8. Has extra convenient hours. _____
9. Offers discounts for volume. _____
10. Solves problems your customers haven't thought of. _____
11. Courteous plus attitude. _____
12. Asks about customers' health and welfare, "How are things going?" _____
13. Constantly improving policies or procedures. _____
14. Makes comments that say, "I care." _____
15. Says, "Thank you" to every customer. _____
16. Displays eagerness to solve problems. _____
17. Shows willingness to help another employee. _____
18. Gives complete attention to customer. _____
19. Cleanliness of business. _____
20. Appearance of employees. _____
21. Has a comfortable customer lounge. _____
22. Exceeds the customer's expectation in a common transaction. _____
23. Provides incentives, bonuses or awards to customers. _____
24. Tries new ideas to be better, faster, different. _____
25. Apologizes for inconvenience or problems. _____

MAKE A PLAN AND MEASURE RESULTS

If you can't measure it, you can't control it. Companies track expenses, sales and profit. Likewise, to improve customer satisfaction, you need to measure results from customer surveys and internal plans. This principle of excellence will help you succeed by putting the service ideas into practice.

One medium-sized midwest company began its quality revolution in earnest. They had an all-company meeting to discuss service. Buttons were passed out and a company newsletter was started. After six months, not much had happened. Employees and managers began to think the whole idea was another fad. The president decided to document their efforts. All quality ideas were discussed and put into a quarterly plan. The results were amazingly positive. Employee morale improved. Complaints decreased; repeat/referral business increased and profits rose.

APPLICATION 15

In this chapter you've studied the concept of service. Remember these words by Tom Peters (author of *A Passion for Excellence*):

"Listening to customers must become everyone's business. With most competitors moving even faster, the race will go to those who listen (and respond) most intently."

Part I

Distribute the employee survey to your people at a departmental meeting after "moments of truth" and the Customer Service Model, have been discussed. Ask them to fill it out anonymously. Collect the surveys at your meeting.

Part II

Create a written plan for creating superior service. Talk to other managers and employees for ideas. Use the information you gained from customer surveys, the employee survey, and from your own observation. Use the planning form in this chapter as a guide to format the plan. Good luck!

APPLICATION 15 (continued)

Part III

Review the customer surveys that follow. How can you use these or similar surveys in your business? A consultant asked attendees at an Inc. Conference this question, "How many believe that customer satisfaction increases profits?" All 53 leaders said they believed it. Then he asked, "How many survey your customers, then use the information? " Only three did. **To be excellent, survey your customers in the next 30 days. Then do it again 30 days later.**

There are other ways to listen and learn from your customers. Use these methods in the near future too:

- customer interviews
- customer visits
- complaint analysis
- phone surveys
- act like a customer, shop competitors and your own company

Customer Satisfaction: Employee Survey

We provide good service to our customers. In today's competitive environment good isn't good enough. We have to do better to succeed. I need everyone's help to do that. Please give me your views on this survey. You don't need to put your name on it. Thanks.

1. What are we doing right (strengths)?

2. What are we not doing enough of or what should we stop doing?

3. What else can we do to improve our service?

"The greatest enemy of excellence is good."— Zig Ziglar

Customer Satisfaction Plan

Effective dates _____

Area to improve	Action steps	Timeline	Person responsible	Measurement of success
1.				
2.				
3.				
4.				
5.				
6.				
7.				
8.				
9.				
10.				

Summary of results:

Customer Satisfaction Survey

Your feedback is important to us. Below are 25 questions. Please circle your response on the scale for each item. Thanks for your help. (Response scale: 1 = not at all; 2 = to a very little degree; 3 = to a little degree; 4 = to some degree; 5 = to a great degree; 6 = to a very great degree)

Circle
Response

1. To what degree do our personnel have a professional appearance?

1 2 3 4 5 6

2. To what degree is our equipment reliable in fulfilling your requirements?

1 2 3 4 5 6

3. To what degree do our physical facilities convey our customer satisfaction intent?

1 2 3 4 5 6

4. To what degree do we attach importance to "image" as seen by you or other customers?

1 2 3 4 5 6

5. To what degree is our equipment "state of the art" to support customer service?

1 2 3 4 5 6

6. To what degree are we accurate in our transactions with you? 1 2 3 4 5 6

7. To what degree do we place value on problem solving with you?

1 2 3 4 5 6

8. To what degree do we emphasize thoroughness in providing you service?

1 2 3 4 5 6

9. To what degree are our promises to you kept in this organization?

1 2 3 4 5 6

10. To what degree are we dependable in fulfilling our promises to you?

1 2 3 4 5 6

11. To what degree do we provide prompt responses to your requests?

1 2 3 4 5 6

12. To what degree do we convey a willingness to help you? 1 2 3 4 5 6

13. To what degree are we prompt in serving you? 1 2 3 4 5 6

14. To what degree do we solve your problems quickly? 1 2 3 4 5 6

15. To what degree do we effectively respond to product and service complaints?

1 2 3 4 5 6

16. To what degree are our employees knowledgeable about our products?

1 2 3 4 5 6

17. To what degree do our employees instill trust in you that we will meet your needs?

1 2 3 4 5 6

18. To what degree do you trust we will do all we can to make our dealings "hassle free"?

1 2 3 4 5 6

19. To what degree can you count on receiving professional, courteous service when you call?

1 2 3 4 5 6

20. To what degree do we provide individual attention to your needs?

1 2 3 4 5 6

21. To what degree do our employees demonstrate that we care about your problems?

1 2 3 4 5 6

22. To what degree do we effectively listen to your needs?

1 2 3 4 5 6

23. To what degree do our workers "moan and groan" about you, other customers or departments?

1 2 3 4 5 6

24. To what degree are we dependable in fulfilling our promises to you?

1 2 3 4 5 6

25. To what degree can you trust that employees know how to get prompt action for you?

1 2 3 4 5 6

Review:

1. Add up the points for each question and divide by 25 to get a Customer Satisfaction Rating. Compute a rating for each service area by adding up the points for each question and dividing by 5.

   a. Tangibles-questions 1-5
   b. Reliability-questions 6-10
   c. Responsiveness-questions 11-15
   d. Assurance-questions 16-20
   e. Empathy-questions 21-25

2. Use this survey or adjust the words to make it specific for your organization.

3. This survey is used with permission of Doug Watsabaugh. For more information, or for help with a computerized version, contact: Doug Watsabaugh & Associates, 6328 Fallbrook Rd., Eden Prairie, MN 55344.

Sample Survey

How Good Were We?

	Yes	No
1. Were we courteous?	____	____
2. Were we prompt?	____	____
3. Did we answer all your questions?	____	____
4. Were we correct in our paperwork?	____	____
5. Are the facilities neat?	____	____
6. Did we offer you other service options?	____	____

7. Overall, how satisfied are you? Circle one.

Very satisfied   5   4   3   2   1   Very dissatisfied

Comments:

The Customer Satisfaction Goal Line

Customer Satisfaction Our #1 Priority

Our customers define what's right for them.

I listen, think and respond with care.

What I do makes the difference.

The service strategy statement above is the way to handle every "moment of truth" with customers.

Every employee must cross the customer satisfaction goal line. It will take a team effort to succeed, just as it does in football. It will determine whether you survive and stay profitable in the years ahead. It's the right way to do business in the marketplace today.

Research has found that people usually focus on their weaknesses and think negatively. Is it any wonder that there is a great deal of skepticism about companies and people who step away from the crowd and declare worthy goals? People reject goal lines because they have none. Instead they react out of fear with their words: how, if only, and why. You must guard against these reactions. Here are a few suggestions to help.

Think "what" not "how"

President Kennedy stated to the world in 1961 that we would "put a man on the moon and return safely to earth by the end of the decade." Kennedy didn't know how. He wasn't a chemist or engineer. He left the know-how to NASA. He knew the "what" and took the first step by sharing a vision and providing money. And it happened!

What did Kennedy do that was different? He decided on the what, didn't worry about how, and moved with faith toward the goal line. Dr. Charles Garfield's research at Performance Science Institute in California supports this. He interviewed 1,500 peak performers and discovered that among other attributes, they set goals for themselves and their companies and crystallized the image of success in their minds. Then they took the necessary risks to get there.

Companies or people *without* goals build a different scenario. They don't believe in their best, and they put out fires all day. The how is their worry and they blame "reasons" for their lack of achievement. The next time you worry or have stress instead of results, take a break. Remember to focus on the customer. See that clearly in your mind.

It's not "if only" but "what now"

Two men were visiting. The first asked the second, "What's the dumbest thing you ever did?" The second replied, saying that he could fill a book with the dumb things he'd done. The first topped that by suggesting he could fill three volumes. The second chided, "That's the difference between us."

"If only I said this." "If only I did that." "If only things were different." Too often we play the "if only" game, remembering, hanging onto and worrying about the stupid things we did or mistakes we made. Have you ever caught yourself doing that after a sale? Or before you talked to a customer? Are you left with an overwhelming sense of confidence? Probably not.

The only thing you can change is your attitude and action about what is now. Everyone makes mistakes. Learn from them and move on. Try this experiment. When you get caught in the "if only" game, call time out. Review the service strategy statement above and take the next step. See if you don't begin to build more rapport with customers. And enjoy your work more.

Don't ask "why" say "why not"

- Why didn't I close the sale?
- Why are they so angry?
- Why do employees have bad attitudes?
- Why isn't this thing taking off?
- Why am I blamed?

Do you find yourself saying things like that? If you do, fear is creeping up on you as sure as spring is coming. Either you're losing sight of the customer satisfaction goal, or you don't care.

Take time to review the goal. Bobby Kennedy stated, "Some people see things as they are and ask why. I see things that aren't and ask, why not?"

Why not more than satisfy customers? Why not follow up on the sale or service? Why not cooperate with others? Why not have pride in your work? Why not do a better job each day? Why not give added value? Someone wrote, "Our greatest fear is the fear of being ourselves."

Managers who succeed go for the goal. Then know that it saves money to keep an old customer rather than find a new customer. Excellent managers know the power of word-of-mouth advertising. They focus on the customer. Superior service is their goal. They achieve it and they enjoy the admiration and respect of others, including their competitors.

PART 4

MANAGING YOUR TIME
FOR RESULTS

(How to Save Two Hours Every Day)

CASE REVIEW IV: The Best or the Worst

Dennis is the manager for a non-profit organization. His job is to coordinate the assistance given to disadvantaged youth. His organization helps them finish their educations and find jobs.

Dennis is socially good with people and people like him. He communicates well and is sincere. However, he's always losing things. He forgets to return phone calls. Decisions are put off to the very last minute. He makes promises he can't deliver on. His subordinates don't know what to expect and lack direction. He keeps notes and schedules in three or four places and often misses or arrives late for appointments. Although he has a kind heart, there is turmoil in his organization.

1. Is Dennis one of the best or worst managers? Why?

_____

_____

_____

2. What are three to five character traits you see in Dennis?

_____

_____

_____

IDENTIFY YOUR TIME WASTERS

"He who gains victory over other men is strong, but he who gains a victory over himself is all powerful."
—Lao Tse

You can't manage your time any better; you can manage yourself better. Everyone receives 168 hours a week. Time is a constant. It's what you do with the time that matters. This chapter's key to excellence is self-management, not time management. In addition, you'll review techniques for results, but more importantly, you'll set yourself up for action. Finally, this isn't about working harder. It's about working smarter. By following the principles and applications in this chapter, you can literally save yourself two hours a day.

If you were to compare yourself to a boat, which one of the following describes you? (Check one):

_____ Yacht
_____ Ocean liner
_____ Tugboat
_____ Speedboat
_____ Sailboat

In the box below, write in why you chose the boat you did.

Note: Remember, your perception of the world and self is often different than what others see. Your self-esteem is the first step to successful living. In other words, how you see yourself today determines your tomorrow. No matter what boat you picked, it relates to how you perceive yourself moving forward in life. Is your image appropriate? If not, change it! If it is, how can it be improved? Begin this chapter with an open mind, and be ready to change.

IDENTIFY YOUR TIME WASTERS (continued)

Many managers say, "I don't have time to plan ahead, deal with customers, counsel employees or keep up with paperwork." Any manager worthy of her position doesn't use these excuses. If time pressures are too great, don't make excuses, take action:

- delegate
- say no
- work longer
- establish priorities
- get help

In other words, an excellent manager understands she is accountable for results, so she makes things happen.

How do you handle time pressures? In the exercise on the next page, analyze your major time wasters. Then be prepared to act, to change for the better.

Time Wasters

Directions: Check the appropriate personal response for each item. Are the items always, sometimes, or never true for you?

	Always	Sometimes	Never
1. Do you attend many *meetings* that don't matter?	____	____	____
2. Do you *procrastinate* often?	____	____	____
3. Do you have too many *phone conversations*?	____	____	____
4. Do *drop-in visitors* interrupt you?	____	____	____
5. Do you lack specific daily *plans*?	____	____	____
6. Do you lack specific and measurable business *goals*?	____	____	____
7. Does it seem as though most of your time is spent on *routine and trivia*?	____	____	____
8. Do you have a *cluttered desk*?	____	____	____
9. Are you *indecisive*?	____	____	____
10. Do you seem to regularly have *afternoon drowsiness*?	____	____	____

11. Does it seem you have to *repeat instruc-
    tions or directions* to subordinates?   ____   ____   ____

12. Does *paperwork* take up a big part of
    your day?   ____   ____   ____

13. Do you *try to do it all* to succeed?   ____   ____   ____

14. Do unexpected *problems* cause you to react
    and divert other priorities?   ____   ____   ____

15. Are you a member of the *coffee klatsches*?   ____   ____   ____

16. Do you lack *specific blocks of time* to work
    on priorities?   ____   ____   ____

APPLICATION 16

Any items you checked always are limiting your *effectiveness*. Pick
one area and write it in the box below. Be determined to minimize
its effect as a timewaster. See the next page for ideas on how to
form new habits for each timewaster. Work at it for 30 days and
evaluate the results in the box below. Keep working at it until a new
good habit is formed, then pick a new timewaster to eliminate.

Timewaster—   Date _____

30-day Evaluation—

Timewaster—   Date _____

30-day Evaluation—

IMPLEMENT TIMEGAINERS

"To love is to love time.
Time is the stuff life is made of."
—Ben Franklin

"Time is the continuum in which events succeed
one another from past through present to future."
—Webster's Dictionary

"The more time we spend on planning a project, the less
total time is required for it. Don't let today's busy work
crowd planning time out of your schedule."
—Edwin Bliss, *Getting Things Done*

To be effective in managing your time, you must be willing to do that which an unsuccessful manager won't do. To overcome your timewasters, you must use a number of timegainers. Sixteen timegainers are described in the next few pages. Before you decide which to implement, read these three Laws to Time Management.

Laws To Time Management

1. *Real time management is self-management.* You can't manage time; you can manage yourself. Time is constant, 168 hours a week. What *you* do with your time is the secret to getting more done.

2. *To manage yourself better, you must be willing to change.* New habits must replace old habits. Fold your arms. Notice which arm is tucked in. Fold your arms again; this time have the other arm tucked in. How does it feel? Uncomfortable? Change is usually uncomfortable at first. With persistence and repetition, this can be overcome. If you always folded your arms the second way, it would become natural.

3. *The key to self-management is to manage your response to an event.* Good time managers are good at controlling their responses to events they can't control. Do the events exercise on the next page.

Events Exercise

Directions: Read each of the activities that are listed. Ask yourself how much control you have for how or when things like this happen. Then check (✓) the appropriate response. (Check one for each area.)

	No Control	Some Control	Complete Control
1. Subordinate sickness	____	____	____
2. Customer complaints	____	____	____
3. Drop-in visitors	____	____	____
4. Phone interruptions	____	____	____
5. Bosses' priorities	____	____	____
6. Routine & trivia	____	____	____
7. Meetings	____	____	____
8. Traffic jams	____	____	____
9. Long-winded speakers	____	____	____
10. Weather-related problems	____	____	____
11. Employee personal problems	____	____	____
12. Other people's accidents	____	____	____
13. Death	____	____	____
14. Mechanical breakdowns	____	____	____
15. Your planning efforts	____	____	____
16. Your attitude	____	____	____

IMPORTANT!

Although you can't control or have limited control over many events you experience, you always have control how you respond. How you respond depends on your attitude and your willingness to plan. Make a commitment to use the timegainer techniques on the next pages. You'll get more done in less time, be respected for it, and feel good about it, too!

Implement Timegainers

1. Meetings

Only attend meetings that are useful. Only hold a meeting with an agenda. Start on time, be on time, end on time. Delegate meetings to others. Schedule meetings back to back.

2. Procrastination

Set deadlines, and specific priorities. Promise results in writing to another person. Break large projects into smaller ones.

3. Phone Interruptions

When working on top projects/problems, have calls screened. Get out of your office. Limit the time of routine phone contacts.

4. Drop-in Visitors

Stand and talk to the visitor. Explain that you'd love to talk but can't now. Be direct, but polite. Close your door.

5. Daily Plan

Use one, but don't get too complicated. This technique itself is worth your investment in this book. Every day, evening or morning, write down six things to do. Start with #1 and work at one at a time. Don't worry if you don't finish. Transfer unfinished items to the next day.

6. Goals

Set business and personal goals. It works to help make you more productive. Lack of direction wastes time and effort. Goal setting is one of the greatest success secrets of all-time.

7. *Routine and Trivia*

Do trivia or routine by schedule. Don't do it whenever it pops up. Save junk mail, phone calls, or reading for times you have lower energy or non-prime time.

8. *Cluttered Desk*

One manager of a major clothing retailer had only 3 pieces of paper on his desk at a time. Each stood for a priority he needed to handle. He did one at a time. Clean off your desk, put anything you can out of sight so you're not distracted. Do one priority at a time.

9. *Indecision*

Gather information and act. Take calculated risks; that's a manager's job. And, keep others appropriately involved or informed of your decisions.

10. *Directions*

Be specific and if you need to, ask subordinates to paraphrase or repeat your instructions back to you. Always follow up to check results. If you have to, put instructions in writing.

11. *Paperwork*

Call, don't put it in a memo. Handle mail only once. Write notes on letters/memos and return them, instead of doing another letter or memo. Anytime you pick up a piece of paper, do something with it, including filing it or throwing it away.

12. *Afternoon Drowsiness*

Take a walk at noon. Work out at a health club. Eat a light lunch.

Implement Timegainers (continued)

13. Try to Do It All

Focus on the 20% of your tasks that yield 80% of your results. Delegate to others. Say no sometimes. And, give yourself a break once in awhile. You'll end up being more effective.

14. Unexpected problems

Handle them swiftly if necessary. Don't fret or worry about it. You're not a prophet and *you can't plan for everything.* Make sure you're training employees to solve their own problems. Ask, "What are you going to do?" Don't accept problems they can solve.

15. Coffee Klatsches

Ask yourself, "Am I committed to excellence?" If you are, then skip the coffee klatsches. Be sociable some other time.

16. Interruptions

When working on priorities, have your calls screened. Close your door or work in a different location. Establish quiet hours and get things done during the day. You don't always have to work longer to do this.

USE SUCCESSFUL SELF-MANAGEMENT STRATEGIES

Talent, information, and desire are not enough to be successful in management. Change in self-perception and behavior is required, especially in implementing time management techniques. But don't worry. Big changes aren't usually required. It's the little things, if changed, that begin to make a difference. Everyone has comfort zones and blind spots. For example, quickly count the f's in this sentence:

Finished files are the result of years of scientific study of a few dedicated experts.

How many f's did you get? Most count 5; some 6, and a few, 7 (on the first try). There are 7 f's in the sentence. Sometimes we miss the obvious. Read aloud the sentence in each illustration below.

Did you just read the sentences as you remember them? Notice each has an extra word—a, the, the. Most people don't see this the first time.

What are you missing that is right in front of you? Sometimes it's solutions to present problems, ideas, and answers to future issues. What you need is often in front of you but you don't see or use it. Why? It happens to everyone. It has much to do with blinders you put on caused by the beliefs you've learned over the years.

- I can't change!
- I am what I am!
- I'm not that kind of person.
- That's me.
- I always do it this way; it has worked before.

USE SUCCESSFUL
SELF-MANAGEMENT STRATEGIES (continued)

Excellent managers have their problems; however, they are more willing to change or try new things to get results. If it makes sense, they will shed old habits and beliefs as easily as leaves fall from trees in the autumn.

Successful self-management requires you to:

- expand your comfort zone
- build positive beliefs
- increase your productivity
- be satisfied with your life

Expand Your Comfort Zone

All of us put blinders on to our self-imposed limitations. Don't stay a creature of habit. To expand our potential, all managers need:

1. *Feedback*—positive and negative; ask for it!
2. *New ideas*—try different methods; brainstorm.
3. *Failures*—Andrew Carnegie said the way to succeed is to fail more.
4. *Change*—make a new habit or action step and stay with it for 30 days.

Build Positive Beliefs

You do want to increase your performance, energy, and success, don't you? Never forget that talent, knowledge, and desire aren't enough to achieve that. You have to change your beliefs as well. Your beliefs affect your attitude. Your attitude determines if you use your talent, knowledge, and desire.

Here's how to build positive beliefs:

1. Focus on positive results. Sounds simple, but psychologists tell us 85% of our thoughts are negative.
2. Use mental rehearsal. Preplay positive results on sales, goals, and customer contacts.
3. Try self-talk or affirmations. Take time to put positive affirmations in your mind. Do positive in, positive out (PIPO); not garbage in, garbage out (GIGO).

Try affirmations like these:

- I am an *excellent* manager!
- I am healthy and fit!
- I communicate well and with sincerity!

Write a few of your own affirmations. Make them present tense, positive and about yourself.

Increase Your Productivity

Most managers spend most of their time on crises and fires. Not enough time is spent on organizing, planning, marketing, tracking, communicating, training, and motivating. Your true payoff activities involve these functions. Be a pro; make the time to get them done. Eliminate the word "can't" and in the words of Winston Churchill, "Never give up; never, never give up." Implement these peak performance techniques:

1. *Follow a personal management system*—for organization, scheduling, goal tracking, and time management. Suggested programs are Daytimer, Day Runner, Time File, and Time Design. Each includes these key elements:

   a) yearly overview calendar
   b) monthly overview calendar
   c) daily calendar (to do list, calls, and appointments)
   d) telephone log
   e) notes section

   Find one planner and use it. Don't use two or three; you'll be ineffective. Also, if it's important, write it down (meeting, ideas, activity, goal). Initiate this concept in a personal planner and you'll literally save an hour a day.

2. *Write goals and action plans.* Again, if it isn't written down, it's not important to you. All great achievers are great planners. Chance favors the prepared mind. This will be reviewed more in the last chapter.

3. *Keep learning.* Read, listen to tapes, and take courses on management. No matter how successful you are now, you will limit yourself if you stop learning. This also will be discussed more in the last chapter.

Be Satisfied with Your Life

This involves living each moment to the fullest. It's important to plan for the future and to get things done. To be successful also means self-development. However, it's easy to get trapped by a whirlwind or grind and never enjoy or appreciate who you are or what really is important.

Remember these ideas as well:

- Do what you love.
- Nurture your relationships.
- Do nothing sometimes.
- Have alone time.
- Help others.

HIRING THE BEST PEOPLE

(How to Select the Best People for Your Team)

CASE REVIEW V: The Best or the Worst

Tim is a sales manager and has 15 salespeople reporting to him. He's always looking for good salespeople, although he never advertises an opening. His turnover rates are 8 to 10 times below industry averages. The reasons include: he's very selective in whom he hires, his company uses a multiple-interview process, he sets goals, and he reviews progress every month with every salesperson. He does twice as much training as others and he gets sales results. Salespeople normally don't want to leave his department.

1. Is Tim one of the best or worst managers? Why?

_____

_____

_____

2. What is one thing that Tim does that you could do more of?

_____

_____

_____

THE INTERVIEW

An interview is a lot like a test. Most managers get themselves into trouble with their company or the law because they don't understand this. A test measures how well you know something, or how well you can perform a given task. Isn't that what you're trying to do with an applicant for a job?

The problem is that managers seem to be unprepared for interviews, and they end up giving different tests to different candidates, even for the same position. Besides that, they aren't always sure what criteria they are testing the candidates on. The end results are mismatches between applicants and companies. Both end up losers.

It is imperative that a manager use a structured format or process consistently with every candidate. Also, the process must fit the subject or job. This takes *current* knowledge of the job and preparation to produce a reliable and valid test for all.

Some managers are worried about the legal implications of their selection efforts. Although it seems that people are lawsuit happy today, a structured process for hiring will help protect you. Here are four key steps to adhere to:

1. Prepare for the interview.
2. Set a positive tone with a candidate.
3. Conduct a businesslike interview.
4. Evaluate all information objectively.

These steps are designed to help you identify if the candidate can do the job. It's a basic yet methodical approach that takes time, but can make you and the right person winners in your organization.

What's the next position you'll be hiring for? Write the title of the job in the space below.

If you aren't hiring soon, use your position or pick one you may hire for in the future.

Use the following exercises to help you prepare to select the best person for your job.

PREPARE FOR THE INTERVIEW

The best way to learn is to do something. The next few pages involve three application exercises that will prepare you for your next interview.

APPLICATION 17

Job Description Exercise

In the space below, make a list of all the job duties/responsibilities for the position you expect to fill. There are two reasons to do this before you hire:

1. To rethink what the job is all about. Jobs change over time.
2. To use the list to develop a series of questions to ask in the interview.

Review the example on the next page. Make the list practical and not so structured or formal that it's not useful. Sometimes it's helpful to ask others (employees in similar positions) to make lists, and then compile them.

Note:
1. Review this with the candidate in the interview.
2. Once a person is hired, discuss the job duties/responsibilities list again soon after the person starts working. Use it to begin the process of goal setting discussed in Chapter 1.

APPLICATION 18

Job Skills/Characteristics Exercise

First, list specific job skills that are required to succeed in the position. This could mean ability to use a typewriter, word processor, certain computers, or a specific machine like a punch press. Identify how many years of experience you want.

Second, list 10 to 12 personality characteristics for the ideal candidate. This could include communications skills, punctuality, creative thinker, etc. Review the examples on the next page for samples.

Skills	Characteristics

Note: The candidate must be told of the skills required for the job. Add them to the job duties list and make a one-page description like the sample on page 90. You do not need to show the candidate the personal characteristics list. It's mainly a resource for the interviewer.

Optional: Another list you can use in the interview is a sample goal setting plan for the new candidate. See the sample on page 92.

Job Duties—Salesperson (sample)

1. Conducts sales in an ethical manner.
2. Maintains professional appearance and behavior at all times.
3. Uses a written plan for prospecting and follow-up.
4. Knows the product well.
5. Uses a formal selling process.
6. Follows a systematic process of delivering the product to the customer.
7. Introduces the customer to other personnel.
8. Contacts the customer after the sale.
9. Attends product and sales training meetings from the store and other sources to achieve excellence.

Experience and Skills:

1. Three to five years sales experience, not necessarily industry related.
2. Ability and personality that relates well to people.
3. Goal-oriented and ambitious.
4. A stable work background with little or no job hopping.
5. Two to four years of college, a degree not necessary.

Characteristics of the "Ideal" Salesperson (sample)

Positive attitude

Outgoing personality

Neat and clean appearance

Works well with others

Pleasing personality

Persistent

Has intensity

Goal-oriented

Independent

Creative

Thinks well under pressure

Good work habits

Good communication skills

Trustworthy

Job Goals: Minimum Standards for New Salesperson for the First Three Months (Sample)

1. Makes six to eight sales per month.

2. Follows a daily work plan.

3. 100% sales follow-up.

4. Achieves 90% customer satisfaction rating.

5. Closes 50% of all sales.

6. Logs 100% of all prospects and tracks results.

Preparing a Question List

In the selection process you want to gain as much information as possible to help you make a good decision. The questions you ask fulfill an important role. You can't shoot from the hip and be effective.

A successful manager has a prepared list of questions she wants to ask. An unsuccessful manager just makes up the questions as she goes. By being prepared with a list of questions, you can be more objective as you compare notes and information about different candidates. Again, this process requires a little homework up front. Over time, it is much more effective than winging it.

Two Kinds of Questions

Two major kinds of questions are important to use.

- Behavioral—focuses on whether a candidate has the skill to do a job.
- Informational—covers a variety of basic, job-related topics, performance issues, and the interviewee's story.

Behavioral Questions

Using behavioral questions is like trying to make a movie of the candidate doing the job. You can't always watch the person in an actual situation, live, but you can determine if the candidate has the knowledge to specifically describe how to do a job. The goal is to probe what the candidate can really do. Behavioral questions begin like this:

—Describe a time . . .
—Give me an example . . .
—Tell me how you . . .
—What did you do about . . .
—Hypothetically, how would you handle this situation . . .

What behavioral-oriented questions do you ask? It depends on the job being interviewed for. However, use this guideline:

> Ask behavioral-oriented questions that deal with priorities on the job duties list.

Behavioral Questions (continued)

Here are some examples:

Position: salesperson
Give me an example of your follow-up procedure. Give me the names of three customers whom I can call.

Position: receptionist
Describe to me how you answer a phone, put people on hold, and transfer calls.

Position: manager
Tell me about a specific situation where an employee had poor performance and how you handled it. What were the results?

Position: machine operator
Tell me how you set up a job on XYZ machine.

Position: customer service
What did you do in your last job to organize and use customer complaint information?

In Application 19, write four to six behavioral-oriented questions you will ask a candidate about the position you described earlier.

Informational Questions

Informational questions help you gather additional information that you need about a candidate. Here are some examples:

—What are your strengths? (personal motivations) Weaknesses? (personal awareness)
—What are your goals?
—Why did you leave your last job? (past job information)
—How would you discuss your working relationship with your boss? Co-workers? (relationships with people)
—Why do you want this job? (knowledge of the job and personal motivation)

In Application 19, write four to six informational questions that you will ask a candidate about the position you described earlier.

APPLICATION 19

Make a written list of 8 to 10 questions to ask a candidate about a particular job. Use the list in the interview and take notes. If others are interviewing the candidate, they should have the list also.

SET A POSITIVE TONE WITH THE CANDIDATE

Although setting a positive tone with the candidate sounds elementary, it is crucial to a successful interview. If you can build rapport with the candidate and help relax him, he'll be more open and genuine with you when questioned about specific or sensitive topics. Your payoff is a better indication of the kind of person the candidate really is. The candidate will be better prepared to handle the behavioral questions, which often put a person on the spot. This is okay, because you need to know if the person can do the job and how he'll handle stress.

There are three ingredients to setting a positive tone:

- Create a positive environment.
- Use introductory small talk.
- Give an overview of the interview.

Create a Positive Environment

One manager told a training class that she had high turnover rates. She said she thought this happened because she didn't have much time to hire. Her priority was to keep an eye on production. So she had to interview all candidates at her desk, which was surrounded by a conveyor belt assembly line. She said there was no privacy and many interruptions.

Successful interviews require privacy and no interruptions. Not only does this allow for increased communication but it also helps project a good image for your organization. You're also selling public relations in the selection process.

A positive environment involves many of the items described in an earlier chapter on communicating with others. The concepts apply in hiring as well.

Use Introductory Small Talk

Build rapport with a candidate by talking about a non-business item after introductions. According to research, this projects friendliness. In a matter of minutes you can put the candidate at ease. Use the person's name and make sure the candidate knows your name. If appropriate, offer the person coffee or a soda. Then begin by giving an overview of the interview.

Give an Overview of the Interview

The reason for the overview is to make sure the candidate knows your objective and how you will proceed with the interview.

As simple as it sounds, your objective is to find and hire the best person for the job opening. In the interview you will:

a. Ask questions to gain information about the candidate. Use your question list.
b. Show the job duties/responsibilities list to the candidate and explain the job.
c. Listen to and answer any questions from the candidate.
d. Administer any assessment tools.
e. Close the interview professionally.

- The interview will take 25 to 40 minutes.
- Tell the candidate what the next steps are. Don't leave anyone hanging.

1) Be honest and direct. Explain if the candidate is qualified or not.
2) Send a personal letter (no form letters) for acceptance or rejection of the candidate.
3) Or, call each person and give your decision.

In Application 20, write out how you'll handle each step of the interview process. The difference between winning and losing is that the winners do what others won't do at all or won't do enough of.

APPLICATION 20

Interview Steps

Check each area as you complete your descriptions ($\checkmark$).

Descriptions

1. Create a positive ☐
   environment.

2. Use introductory ☐
   small talk.

3. Give an overview ☐
   of the interview.

4. Ask questions. ☐

5. Show the job ☐
   duties list.

6. Answer questions. ☐

7. Administer ☐
   assessment tools.

8. Close the interview. ☐

Note: Each person who interviews the candidate needs to see this information.

CONDUCT THE INTERVIEW

Successful organizations use a multiple-interview process. In other words, they interview the candidate more than once, and more than one person is involved. One large company interviews candidates seven times and a decision for hire has to be unanimous. Another organization interviews people 25 times, and not surprisingly, the turnover is near zero. A good guideline is to use the rule of 3's. Interview the candidate three times and in three different situations. This process does take more time, but if you get a more valuable employee, it's worth it. By using a multiple-interview process, you'll make better decisions. You'll minimize the effect of personal bias or prejudice. You'll gain more information on the candidate's real qualifications, and you'll reduce the risk of misinterpreting data about a person.

Do Application 21 and rate yourself on a scale of 1 to 5 as to the Do's and Don'ts of interviewing (1 = poor; 5 = excellent). In column A, rate yourself as you have done interviewing in the past. In column B, rate yourself two to three months from now after you have applied the interview steps discussed. Total each column and compare the results. What can you learn or relearn about your efforts?

APPLICATION 21

Do's/Don'ts of Interviewing

Do	Rating A B	Don't
1. Be thoroughly prepared.	__ __	Wing it.
2. Create a positive environment.	__ __	Try to grill or intimidate the candidate.
3. Follow the interview steps.	__ __	Shoot from the hip without a plan.
4. Use introductory small talk and give an overview.	__ __	Act discourteous or rude.
5. Ask pre-planned behavioral/ informational questions.	__ __	Make things up as you go.
6. Listen actively.	__ __	Get easily distracted with interruptions or thoughts.

APPLICATION 21 (continued)

7.	Take notes.	__ __	Rely on your memory.
8.	Control the interview and keep the candidate on track with questions.	__ __	Let the candidate dictate the pace of the interview.
9.	Review the job duties list.	__ __	Leave out information about the job.
10.	Answer questions.	__ __	Minimize or ignore the candidate's questions.
11.	Administer appropriate assessment tools.	__ __	Make decisions solely on "gut" feel.
12.	Use the multiple-interview process for better judgment.	__ __	Rush the selection process.
13.	Avoid the halo/horn effect (based on one piece of information, the candidate is all good or bad).	__ __	Hire based on first impression.
14.	Close every interview professionally.	__ __	Close abruptly and with no explanation of next steps.
15.	Follow up with all applicants.	__ __	Leave people hanging.

EVALUATE ALL INFORMATION OBJECTIVELY

This part of the selection process is critical. Your aim here is to pull together all your facts, compare them to the other interviewers', and then make as objective a decision as possible to hire the best person.

The information you'll have available involves:

Application/resume
- Remember, resumes are sales tools; discount them.
- Is the application neat and complete?
- Look for gaps in employment and any peculiar information.
- Is the education and experience applicable to the job?
- Most candidates can be screened before an interview because of an inadequate background.

Interview
- Is the person on time, neat and appropriate in appearance?
- Take notes on the answers to the questions.
- Also, note how the candidate compares to your personal characteristics list.
- Interview at least three qualified people for the job.

Reference checks
- Most managers are wary of giving out information on reference calls. Call anyway.
- Do two to three reference checks per candidate. It gives you additional information to review.
- Don't call personnel; call the supervisor or manager of a department or co-workers.
  1) Start by giving the name of the candidate and verifying employment dates and the position.
  2) Ask what the candidates' strengths are.
  3) Ask if the candidate has any weaknesses.
  4) Ask if there is anything else you should know about.
  5) Ask if the person would hire the candidate again.
- Read between the lines. If the reference hesitates when she answers, you may need to probe this.
- If you network in your field, you usually will be able to find someone who knows about the candidate.
- Call a person's friends as a reference. Using the process above, one manager called the friend/business associate of a sales applicant. The friend gave information on weaknesses that was important in the final hiring decision.

EVALUATE ALL INFORMATION OBJECTIVELY (continued)

Assessment Tools

Never use assessments as the final decision. Use the results to corroborate or contradict previously-identified information.

Most companies can't afford expensive assessment processes. Two inexpensive tools are recommended and have been used by the author to help in the selection process.

1. **The Wonderlic Personnel Test.** Performance norms have been done on thousands of people. It is a 12-minute test self-administered and scored, that identifies a candidate's ability to read, think, and problem-solve compared to others in similar positions. Contact Wonderlic in Northfield, Illinois, 1-800-323-3742.

2. **Personal Profile System.** It's an inventory, not a test, that helps you identify a person's work or behavioral style, motivational patterns, and potential strengths and weaknesses in relating to others. This is self-administered and scored in 15 to 25 minutes. It enables you to predict if a candidate will match your organization's climate and the behavioral needs of a particular job. It also gives valuable information on how to manage someone. The Personal Profile is not intended to be used as the only determinant of a person's capability to do a job. Contact Carlson Learning Company in Minneapolis, Minnesota, 612-449-2856 for more information.

APPLICATION 22

After you interview the candidate, use the forms below and on the next page to review notes with other interviewers and to compare candidates. The two forms are:

1. *Process Review* form. The purpose is to summarize all the information you gathered on a candidate. Then compare it to the job duties and skills list.

2. *Hiring Evaluation* form. The purpose of this form is to evaluate through ranking how each candidate stacks up compared to the required qualifications.

Process Review

What did you learn about the candidate?

1. Application/resume

2. Interview

3. Reference check

4. Assessment tools

Hiring Evaluation

APPLICANT'S NAME _____ DATE _____

POSITION _____

Qualifications	Importance (Assign each a 1-5 value) 1 = low imp.; 5 = high imp.	Rating 1 = low; 10 = high fit	Evaluation Results Important × Rating
1. Experience			
2. Education			
3. Personal Characteristics			
4. Appearance			
5. References			
6. Other _____			
7. Other _____			

Total Points _____

(Add other qualification if necessary. Use the same qualifications and importance value for candidates applying for same position.)

Manager's Check (check if complete)

1. Application/resume ____
2. 3 interviews   ____
3. 3 references   ____
4. Assessment tools   ____

Comments   (Hired ____   Not hired ____)

What to Look for in a Candidate

When you review a candidate's past experience and education, you want someone with a successful background. Does the candidate show evidence of achievement? Has the candidate increased her income, won awards, received recognition, been involved in activities and improved her position in life? Or, is the past littered with idleness and mediocrity?

A candidate needs to be results-focused also. Does she have examples of getting things done that are memorable and measurable? Does the person speak about increasing sales, developing projects, making things happen? You want someone who will take initiative to be a success. You want a goalsetter and goalgetter.

Another key trait to be attracted to is a sense of urgency. Does the candidate really want to work for you? Is he or she eager to start, or does he or she need a month off? You want someone who is motivated to be part of your team as quickly as possible.

Next, give the candidate the family test. Is the candidate the kind of person who you'd want to be part of your closest family? Can you trust her? Is she friendly and warm? Eliminate candidates who are unethical. Does the candidate bad-mouth competitors or her present company? If she does this about others, she'll do it about you.

Finally, does the candidate want to interview you? Does he show ambition to check you out without being arrogant? Does he ask intelligent questions? You want someone who is self-confident enough to speak up to ask meaningful questions or raise necessary issues.

Take hiring seriously. Excellent managers always have excellent people. A manager influences and gets results through people. Invest the time to hire and you'll obtain the best people. And, it is an investment. The average cost per hire today is around $10,000. To be honest, you can't afford the turnover. Do it right and you'll hire right. You'll actually save yourself time, money and people-problems later.

PART 6

ACHIEVING MANAGERIAL
EXCELLENCE

(Take Your Abilities to Their Limits)

CASE REVIEW VI: The Best or the Worst

Pete has been a manager for about eight years. He has won recognition for profit and sales as a store manager. Over his career he's always made progress. His track record involves success at sales, middle management, and buying and running his own franchise. Although his results are good compared to others, they aren't exceptional.

Pete is known as a tough no-nonsense manager. He sees himself as a motivator and a doer. His management team does it his way with little discussion on issues. He's also known for his tantrums if things are bad. While Pete is successful, his progress seems blocked. In slow times, poor quality products are shipped to make the bottom line looks good. His approach to problems is to do more of the same, harder.

1. What are two or three qualities you see in Pete?

_____

_____

_____

2. Is he an excellent manager? Why or why not?

_____

_____

_____

LEADERSHIP AND MANAGEMENT

Which of the following people would you rate as excellent leaders? Excellent managers? Or both? Check the appropriate box or boxes for each person.

	Excellent Leader	Excellent Manager	Neither Case
1. Ronald Reagan (former U.S. President)	☐	☐	☐
2. Margaret Thatcher (former English Prime Minister)	☐	☐	☐
3. Robert Redford (actor, producer)	☐	☐	☐
4. Donald Trump (businessman)	☐	☐	☐
5. Vince Lombardi (former coach, Green Bay Packers)	☐	☐	☐
6. Abraham Lincoln (former U.S. President)	☐	☐	☐
7. Ted Turner (businessman)	☐	☐	☐
8. Lee Iacocca (chairman, Chrysler Corp.)	☐	☐	☐
9. Jimmy Bakker (PTL fame)	☐	☐	☐
10. George Bush (U.S. President)	☐	☐	☐
11. Harry Truman (former U.S. President)	☐	☐	☐
12. Tommy Lasorda (manager, L.A. Dodgers)	☐	☐	☐
13. Dave Burns (vice president, general manager)	☐	☐	☐
14. Rick Hedberg (Goodyear franchise owner)	☐	☐	☐
15. Rae Barkley (business owner)	☐	☐	☐

Most seminar participants are familiar with the first 12 people on the list. Also, the majority of participants held mixed reactions and opinions about the effectiveness of these people as excellent leaders or managers. Most also had a hard time determining how to rate leadership and management separately. The last three people on the list aren't widely known from a historical or national perspective. They are known in their own businesses in their communities. Each are admired in their fields for achieving excellent results as leaders and as managers, although their recognition has focused on results, not on specific leadership or management skills.

LEADERSHIP AND MANAGEMENT (continued)

Important: How did you rate the list? Please remember these points. You don't have to have your name in the paper or your story and picture in a magazine to achieve excellence. In fact, the best leaders and managers most often come from ordinary people creating extraordinary outcomes in local institutions or businesses across the country. Excellence is learned; no one is born with it. And the differences between leadership and management are most likely slight and probably don't matter. Results are what count the most.

HOW TO USE LEADERSHIP AND MANAGEMENT

Many business experts today have gained media attention by debating whether or not leadership is more important than management. Many books and articles have been published to add fuel to the fire. The key question is, does it matter? What really counts is to be successful directing or guiding the work of others. To do this *you need to lead and manage.*

Leadership is more of an influencing function designed to motivate a group to put forth its best efforts. A leader exhibits these kinds of behavior:

- being a mentor for others
- establishing a work culture
- acting as a resource
- creating opportunities for growth
- being a cheerleader
- challenging others
- setting an overall vision

Management is more of a thinking function designed to implement a team's best effort. A manager initiates these kinds of behaviors:

- instructing others
- organizing work flow
- planning/goalsetting for the group
- supporting activities
- coaching performance
- problem-solving issues
- relating to others daily

The differences between these functions are slight. But little things can spell winning or losing. In the 100-yard dash, a hundredth of a second can mean first place or last place. The leadership function tends to focus on people issues, while the management function tends to focus on task issues. With the competitiveness in the marketplace today, you need to do both functions well to achieve excellence and success.

APPLICATION 23

Part I

Do the Best of the Best exercise on the next page to identify your individual standards of excellence.

Part II

Go back and review the Management Skills Inventory at the beginning of the book (page 3). Which skills and behaviors do you need I to develop? List four to six of the areas on the Development Plan (strengths and weaknesses) and then implement your action steps.

Part III

Review the STAR of Self-Development (page 114) for ideas on how to continue to expand your talents. Also, keep this in mind:

"There is no self-improvement, only increasing in the ability to be all that you already are."—Anonymous

Best of the Best Exercise

Think of two or three times in your career where you did your best work ever. Pick those situations that are your examples of your highest performance. Get a clear mental picture of each event. Replay each experience as if it were a movie. Try to imagine each as clearly as possible; include detail—sounds, colors, surroundings, people, and feelings. Review what happened, how you acted, what you felt and what you achieved. These personal best events are your achievements of excellence. There are lessons to be learned and applied so you can springboard to higher heights. Now, answer the following questions.

1. What are the events?

    a.

    b.

2. Describe each event in detail in terms of what happened.

    a.

    b.

    c.

3. What were your motivations to succeed or act?

4. How did you feel?

5. What influence did you have on others?

6. What key behaviors or strategies did you use?

7. What lessons can you learn or relearn from these experiences?

8. How can you use these lessons today?

Development Plan

Directions: List 4-6 areas (strengths or weaknesses) that need further development. Develop a plan to succeed.

Developmental Area/Goal	Action Steps	Timeline	Evaluation
1. Area: Goal:			
2. Area: Goal:			
3. Area: Goal:			
4. Area: Goal:			
5. Area: Goal:			
6. Area: Goal:			

The STAR of Self-Development
to Increase your Knowledge and Skill

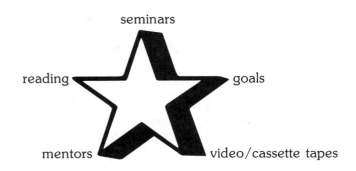

Success Techniques

The STAR Questionnaire

	Yes	No
1. Do you attend 3-4 seminars or more a year to continue your education and training?	☐	☐
2. Do you watch videos or listen to cassette tapes regularly to gain new ideas and information?	☐	☐
3. Do you have goals written on paper that you review regularly?	☐	☐
4. Do you read a book a month in your field?	☐	☐
5. Do you have some mentors (people whom you learn from) that you talk to regularly?	☐	☐

"If you want to be exceptional, do exceptional things. The difference between winners and losers is that the winners do what losers won't do at all or won't do enough."

IMPROVE YOUR PROBLEM-SOLVING SKILLS

A significant part of a manager's job is problem solving. An excellent manager differentiates himself from the mediocre by taking initiative to get things done. Excellent managers take responsibility to work at preventing problems or improving current processes or procedures as opposed to waiting until the problems move from a mild irritation to a major burden.

There is a story about a new manager who asked a veteran manager the secret of his success. The veteran replied, "Making good decisions." The new manager then asked for an idea on how to make good decisions. The veteran responded, "Good decisions come from experience." The eager rookie asked another question about how to get experience. The veteran declared, "Experience comes from risk-taking." The rookie then wanted to know what happens when you take risks. The veteran answered by saying, "Bad decisions."

Some organizations have daily management styles entitled:

- managing by the seat of your pants
- crises management

Certainly there are moments when the working environment becomes chaotic. A manager needs to ask: "Is it chaotic because we're busy or is it because we don't know what's going on?"

With a proactive approach to solving problems, a manager can make her life and the life of her employees much more satisfying on the job.

Read through the story on the next page quickly and write down an answer immediately in the blank by A.

Then read the story a second time but go through it more thoughtfully. Think about the story and analyze what happened. Then write your answer in the blank by B.

The Clothing Store Story

A women went into a clothing store to buy a $34 pair of slacks. She handed the salesperson a $50 bill. It was late in the day and the salesperson didn't have any $1 bills. She took the $50 bill and went next door to the bank service center where she exchanged it for 50 $1 bills. She gave the customer her change. Early the next morning the bank manager and a police officer came to the salesperson and said, "This is a counterfeit $50 bill." The salesperson apologized and explained to both of them what had happened the day before. The salesperson took back the phony bill and gave the bank manager five good $10 bills. Not counting the cost of the slacks, how much money did the clothing store owner lose?

A _____

B _____

The Problem-Solving Process and Techniques

Success in problem solving requires a thoughtful long-term approach, not a quick-fix short-term approach. In the clothing store story, the way you came up with your first answer is similar to the way most managers solve problems—do it quickly and get it done. Their motto often is, "We never have time to do it right the first time. We always have to find the time to do it over again." What answer did you get the first time? $50, $66, $4? The second time through most get the correct answer, which is $16.

A problem-solving approach makes the answer obvious.

Any manager who has been on the job more than a year has a major hurdle to overcome. Once a manager knows a job he becomes an expert. An expert is paid to have the answers and this inhibits the problem-solving process.

APPLICATION 24

Think of a problem you face in your organization. It could be a performance problem or a quality problem. Use the Problem-Solving Process to think through why the problem occurs. Write out in detail your ideas, use the Problem-Solving Process outline that is provided. Do this yourself. Next, get a group of employees together and go through the steps, gaining their input. Use the problem-solving techniques as methods to help obtain their involvement and participation.

After the exercise, take notes on what you've learned about the process.

What I learned or relearned is . . .

The Problem-Solving Process

I. Identify the problem.
   a. Don't assume anything.
   b. Seek causes, not only symptoms.
   c. Ask questions to understand and clarify.
   d. Take notes.

II. State all the facts.
   a. Write everything down.
   b. Gather as much information as possible.
   c. Organize a flow chart or chronological timeline to illustrate what happens.

III. List possible solutions and outcomes.
   a. Identify three solutions and outcomes.
   b. Check your perceptions with others.
   c. Use input from others.
   d. Be creative and brainstorm ideas.

IV. Pick a solution and act.
   a. Do something.
   b. There isn't always one best action.
   c. Don't be afraid to fail.

V. Follow-up.
   a. Monitor and measure progress.
   b. Follow through on agreement.
   c. Try again and start over.
   d. Reorganize positive results.

Problem-Solving Techniques

Open-ended questions

What...?

Where...?

When...?

Why...?

Who...?

Which...?

How...?

Purpose: Designed to stimulate conversation and ideas. What questions do you need to ask about your problem?

_____

_____

_____

_____

Closed-ended questions

Is...?

Are...?

Do...?

Does...?

Have...?

Has...?

Can...?

Will...?

Shall...?

Purpose: Designed to clarify a conversation or to focus on specifics. Write a couple of examples for your problem solving.

_____

_____

_____

_____

_____

_____

Directives

"Tell me more about..."

"Explain that again..."

"Talk more about..."

Purpose: Designed to direct a conversation in a certain direction. What are some tangents you or your group could get sidetracked on?

Problem-Solving Techniques (continued)

Listening Check

"If I understand you correctly, what you're saying is . . ."

Purpose: Designed to verify or clarify what is being said.

"So the problem began when . . ."

"What I hear you saying is . . ."

"Let me see if I have this right . . ."

Summary Statements

"In summary it seems that . . ."

Purpose: Designed to recap a meeting so everyone has a similar perception of the problem.

"We've agreed to the following . . ."

Other Techniques

1. *Verbal cues*

Purpose: Designed to express interest and involvement in conversation.

"I see."

"Hmmm."

"Uh-huh."

"That's interesting."

"I can understand that."

"Yes."

2. *Non-verbal cues*

Nod

Eye contact

Stand straight, lean forward

Arms at side

Take notes

Mirroring/matching

APPLICATION 25

Choose a problem you are currently facing and follow the process below.

I. Identify the problem.

II. State all the facts.

III. List at least three possible solutions and outcomes.

IV. Pick a solution and act.

V. Follow-up.

MASTER STRESS MOTIVATION

There are two kinds of stress: eustress and distress. Eustress is good stress; it's what gives you right attitudes and the motivation to be effective. Distress is negative and harmful; it's what causes pain and disease. Do you have more eustress or distress in your life? All excellent managers are hardy; in other words, they take care of themselves so they stay effective.

According to Dr. Hans Selye, the father of stress research, stress is the body's non-specific response to a demand placed on it. That means different events create different levels of stress in people depending on how they have learned to handle it. For example, a job performance confrontation with an employee creates different stress levels for manager A and employee A as well as for manager B and employee B. The key to creating stress motivation is to first be aware of your body's response to potential stressful situations and second, to implement strategies that eliminate the effect of distress.

Do you use any of these strategies? Check each that applies:

Yes

1. Learn and use stress-reducing techniques such as massage, relaxation, and visualization. ☐

2. Stay fit by exercising at least 3 times a week. ☐

3. Watch your diet. Eat less sugar, salt and fat. Eat balanced meals with more fiber. ☐

4. Help others through charitable or volunteer organizations. ☐

5. Nurture your relationships by taking the time to be together with friends and family. ☐

6. Take care of your spiritual needs. ☐

7. Leave the stressful situation or change your attitude about it. ☐

Note: Do Application 26, on distress appraisal. Also, identify what you can learn/relearn from the activity, There is a delicate balance to maintain to help yourself achieve optimum performance. You need to challenge yourself so you don't "rust out" or underutilize and lose your capabilities. You also need to be careful of overdoing it so you don't "burnout." Peak performance results when the stress you create everyday helps you accomplish worthy objectives while maintaining a healthy lifestyle, positive relationships and an optimistic outlook on life.

APPLICATION 26

Distress Appraisal

Directions: Rate yourself on these items as follows: 5 = strongly agree to 1 = strongly disagree. Circle one number for each.

1.	I worry about losing my job.	1	2	3	4	5
2.	I doubt my ability to do my job successfully.	1	2	3	4	5
3.	Office politics make it hard to be effective.	1	2	3	4	5
4.	My deadlines and timelines are overwhelming.	1	2	3	4	5
5.	I feel more agitated and tired than normal.	1	2	3	4	5
6.	I feel my work has no meaning or importance.	1	2	3	4	5
7.	It's hard to get motivated for work each day.	1	2	3	4	5
8.	I lack the support I need on the job.	1	2	3	4	5
9.	I'm unclear about my accountabilities and responsibilities.	1	2	3	4	5
10.	The quantity of work expected of me interferes with the quality of my efforts.	1	2	3	4	5
11.	I have limited input into my job's goals.	1	2	3	4	5
12.	Conflicting values and expectations are common in my job.	1	2	3	4	5
13.	It's hard to trust anyone at work.	1	2	3	4	5
14.	My job regularly interferes with my family life.	1	2	3	4	5
15.	I don't believe in the company's method of handling people.	1	2	3	4	5
16.	I get limited recognition for my efforts.	1	2	3	4	5
17.	The conflicting demands of my job are irritating.	1	2	3	4	5
18.	I have to sacrifice my integrity to be accepted at my job.	1	2	3	4	5
19.	My job is deadended with no advancement opportunities.	1	2	3	4	5
20.	I'm so busy that I can't get all my work done.	1	2	3	4	5

Total _____

MASTER STRESS MOTIVATION (continued)

Important: If you have 50 or more points, chances are your work is creating extraordinary distress in your life.

If you have 50 or fewer points, you're probably handling the stress on the job effectively (although this review is relative, depending on specific responses to specific situations).

In either case, what can you learn or relearn about yourself? What stress strategies are you using or can you use to limit distress?